SELECT POEMS OF

S. T. COLERIDGE

Please return to 234

WITHDRAWN

SELECTED POEMS OF

SAMUEL TAYLOR
COLERIDGE

Edited with an introduction
and Notes
by

JAMES REEVES

HEINEMANN

LONDON

Heinemann Educational Books Ltd
LONDON EDINBURGH MELBOURNE AUCKLAND TORONTO
HONG KONG SINGAPORE KUALA LUMPUR NEW DELHI
NAIROBI JOHANNESBURG LUSAKA IBADAN
KINGSTON

ISBN 0 435 15021 9

S. T. COLERIDGE 1772–1834

Published by
Heinemann Educational Books Ltd
48 Charles Street, London W1X 8AH
Printed in Great Britain by Morrison & Gibb Ltd
London and Edinburgh

CONTENTS

INTRODUCTION

SAMUEL TAYLOR COLERIDGE was born on 21st October 1772 in the Devon village of Ottery St. Mary, where his father was vicar and master of the grammar school. He was the youngest of John Coleridge's nine sons. Although he afterwards spoke of unkindnesses received as a child, his roots in Ottery were deep. His visits in later life were not frequent or regular, but he kept up an intermittent correspondence with some at least of his brothers, although he was regarded as something of a black sheep in the Coleridge family. Whether or not he was actually maltreated, he was certainly one of those odd children who, perhaps from some deep-seated maladjustment to the society around them, are driven in upon themselves and find their most satisfying reality in tales and romances. Coleridge later attributed the beginnings of the ill-health which afflicted him all his life to some sort of rheumatic complaint caused by exposure to cold and wet when he was six. It was perhaps also by a sort of instinctive loyalty to the place of his birth that he retained all his life a thick west-country accent, which was noticed by visitors in London when he was over fifty.

When Coleridge was nine, his father died, and like other sons of the clergy in need of financial support he was sent as a boarder to Christ's Hospital in London. He remained there from 1782 to 1791. He had already something both of the attraction and the failings of a spoilt child. His mother doted on him, as had his father; and this early favouritism had probably aroused the jealousy and antagonism of one at least of his brothers. He was introspective, and sought solitude, yet the constant desire for love and attention had caused him to develop the power to charm others—a power that never left him, that aroused excessive expectations and demands, and made him assume obligations towards others which he could not fulfil.

The boarding school system, based as it was on the tradition of 'charity', was harsh and repressive. By present standards schools were hopelessly understaffed, so that little supervision could be exercised over the treatment of younger and more sensitive boys by their elders. At first Coleridge suffered intense loneliness and homesickness; he took refuge in dreams, and under the mild sway of Matthew Field, master of the lower school, he seems to have been regarded as something of a dullard. Later, in the upper school, under the supervision of the redoubtable Charles Boyer, he began to develop those intellectual powers for which he was soon to become widely known. Boyer was a savage disciplinarian but, by the standards of the time, a good teacher. Coleridge never ceased to be grateful for the stern and exacting scholarship with which he prepared the older boys for entrance to the universities. Intelligent and sensitive boys often prefer a stern disciplinarian, so long as he is also a scholar, to one more easy-going, since the latter, by encouraging idleness, allows the stronger and less intelligent boys to indulge in the bullying which he is too lazy to check. Boyer did not suffer fools gladly, but Coleridge was not a fool. On the contrary, his intellectual precocity and his engaging manner of holding forth on abstruse philosophical questions earned him the respect of his fellows and the admiration of strangers. He was of striking and attractive appearance, with his dark, untidy hair, his compelling eyes, and the animation and brilliance of his features, which reflected the intelligence working within. Lamb, who was his junior at Christ's Hospital, later compared him in retrospect to the young Pico della Mirandola, philosopher of the Italian Renaissance.

At school Coleridge was befriended by a senior boy, Thomas Middleton, who, on leaving to go up to Cambridge, gave him as a parting present a copy of the poems of William Lisle Bowles. The importance of these to Coleridge was less in any intrinsic merit they possessed than in the liberating influence they exercised on his own latent poetic powers. They seemed to offer an alternative to the mechanical and artificial verse of the followers of Pope and Gray, which at that time represented the current fashion in poetry.

Coleridge in his turn acted as friend and protector to a younger boy, John Evans, to whose home he became a frequent visitor. Here he met Mary Evans, with whom he formed a friendship at once familiar and romantic. During his years at Cambridge the attachment deepened into love and was the occasion of a sustained agony of indecision. From October 1791 until December 1794, with one protracted period of absence, Coleridge was at Jesus College, Cambridge. His rooms were on the ground floor, and his tendency to rheumatism was aggravated by the damp. It was soon after his residence at Cambridge began that the first mention of a recourse to opium as a narcotic occurs. Opium, or laudanum, was at that time widely used as a means of deadening pain, but little was known about its extremely harmful effects as a habit-forming drug. Of more immediate importance, however, was another factor in Coleridge's temperament which decisively established itself at Cambridge—his incapacity to organize his life, to direct his powers for any length of time to a single object. He had one of the liveliest, most impressionable and most discursive minds of which we know anything; in whatever direction it turned, it seemed as if he were bound to follow. He was unable to concentrate, for the sake of academic advancement, on what he conceived as the dull and pedantic discipline of the traditional classical curriculum; instead, his interest turned to philosophy, to æsthetics, to modern politics. This is scarcely to be wondered at. Left-wing politics—Radicalism or Jacobinism as it was then called—was in the air. 1789 was the year of the fall of the

Bastille, an event which Coleridge, like other young men of intelligence and spirit, had hailed as the momentous and decisive occurrence it undoubtedly was. The 1790's, like the 1930's, were one of the most intensely political decades in modern history. It seemed as if the inveterate despotism of the old order in Europe had been triumphantly challenged, and as if nothing could prevent the destruction of tyranny and the establishment of liberty for all those groaning under oppression. Young men could no more avoid being involved in political discussion in the days of Robespierre and Napoleon than in those of Hitler. Coleridge's rooms in Jesus became a meeting-place for men of eager and enquiring mind, who were intoxicated by his brilliance and eloquence. He loved an audience and never tired of talking, giving generously and freely of his intellectual wealth. Coleridge's earliest admirers indulged him by taking it for granted that he would, sooner or later, produce some marvellous work of intellect, no one was very sure what. Yet in hoping so much, and in constantly flattering him with their eager attention, they indulged the very tendency to inaction, to mere speculation, to which he was fatally prone. Had he been less free and open-hearted, had he been more calculating, more self-regarding in the management of his mental capital, he might have become a brilliant lawyer, an influential adminis-trator, a political thinker of wide and lasting fame. But essen-tially he did not want to be any of these things: although, like most—perhaps all—good poets, he was interested in being happy, in the good life, the re-establishment of paradise lost. In many poets there is a latent man of action, inhibited by the fascination of thought, of dreams, of contemplation, and by the apparent uselessness or inadequacy of any specific course of action. To the man who can envisage great ends, all possible means are apt to seem insufficient. Only in the world of the imagination is the poet supremely free and effective. With regard to the management of practical life, Coleridge was tragically ineffective. At Cambridge he got into debt, and his material difficulties so oppressed him that towards the end of 1793 he escaped from material problems by going up to London and enlisting as a trooper in the Light Dragoons under the alias of Silas Tomkyn Comberbache. He was an inefficient soldier, but won instant popularity with his fellow troopers, and his kindness and sympathy made him a successful hospital orderly.

His desperate course alarmed his relations and friends who persuaded him in April 1794 to obtain his discharge and return to Cambridge. In the summer of 1794 he met Robert Southey, and the two poets became close friends. This friendship was perhaps the most disastrous, as it turned out, that Coleridge ever made. Southey's temperament was diametrically opposed to Coleridge's—he was diligent, prudent, and purposeful. His sense of self-preservation was always well developed. Together they evolved the scheme which came to be known as Pantiso-cracy. This was of considerable importance in Coleridge's life, for it is a symbol both of his fundamental sincerity (the willing-ness to act upon his principles) and of his failure to achieve the practical expression of any of the plans his imagination was so prodigal in projecting. The scheme consisted in the setting up of an ideal community in North America, harmonious, self-supporting, and free from the tyranny of outworn social con-ventions. Ultimately, after irreconcilable differences of opinion about the composition of the expedition and the rules of the proposed society, the scheme died a natural death, but not until Coleridge found himself committed, in the interests of the scheme, to a disastrous marriage.

Robert Lovel, one of the intending Pantisocrats, was engaged to a Miss Mary Fricker, one of the five daughters of a Gloucester manufacturer. It was of course envisaged that each of the male members of the community would take a wife, and Southey became engaged to Edith, another of the sisters. Coleridge entered into an engagement to marry yet another sister, Sara.

She was pretty, and appeared to be amiable and industrious. But Coleridge was not in love with her, and he knew in his heart that they were unsuited. Something like panic, and an incapacity to face the consequences of his undertaking, seized him, and he fled to London, where he stayed at the 'Salutation and Cat' Inn, delighting his younger friend, Charles Lamb, with the charm and excitement of his company. Then, as at all times, Lamb was intoxicated by Coleridge's society and over-stimulated by the infectious enthusiasm of his talk. He was helpless under the fascination of Coleridge, whom he admired and believed in, throughout the darkest days of his later misery. Their friendship suffered one temporary estrangement; but Lamb never ceased to revere Coleridge's genius and to acknow-ledge with profound gratitude his power to enrich and illuminate the experience of all who came under his spell.[1]

In London Coleridge also saw Mary Evans, with whom by this time he was in love. She was his ideal of feminine com-panionship, and if he could have brought himself to abandon Pantisocracy and the engagement to Sara Fricker, he might have made Mary his wife, and so altered the course of his existence.

Early in 1795 Coleridge was back in Bristol, where he soon began a series of lectures on political subjects in order to collect funds for the Pantisocratic venture. He continued to hesitate on the question of marriage with Sara. Southey upbraided him for trifling over his engagement, and Coleridge replied that his 'whole life had been a series of blunders'. The breach with Southey widened as it became clearer to Coleridge that the two were in disagreement about the fundamental principles of

[1] Even in Coleridge's darkest days Lamb remained his loyal friend and staunch advocate. When in 1811 Crabb Robinson ventured to use the expression 'Poor Coleridge', Lamb corrected him. 'He is,' he said, 'a fine fellow in spite of all his faults and weaknesses. Call him Coleridge; I hate *poor,* as applied to such a man. I can't bear to hear such a man pitied.' It was Lamb too who said of him, 'His face when he repeats his verses hath its ancient glory—an Archangel a little damaged.'

Pantisocracy. Southey was unwilling to share his money with the rest of the party, and seemed also to believe in the right of some to have servants. Coleridge would willingly have adopted the communistic principles which inspired the first Christians, but Southey, beneath his republicanism, was in embryo already the traditionalist and Tory man of property he later became. It appeared that, for the sake of her engagement with Coleridge, Sara had rejected two suitors, one at least a man of substance. In October 1795 they were married at St. Mary Redcliffe in Bristol and moved to a cottage in Clevedon. The Pantisocratic dream was over, and Coleridge emerged from it with the wife he had taken for its sake. In November he wrote at great length to Southey, soon to become his brother-in-law, saying that he was happy in his marriage and bitterly reproaching Southey with having betrayed the ideals which had brought them together. Referring to the watered-down plan which Southey had put forward, that of setting up a self-contained agricultural community in Wales as a substitute for the original scheme, he concluded: 'In short, we were to commence Partners in a petty Farming Trade. This was the Mouse of which the Mountain Pantisocracy was at last safely delivered!'

A chance acquaintance described Coleridge at this period as 'a young man of brilliant understanding, great eloquence, desperate fortune, and entirely led away by the feelings of the moment'. He himself admitted that he was deficient in will-power and unable to say 'No' to the repeated entreaties of friends and admirers to follow this or that course. His great need was for regular and remunerative employment. Pantiso-cracy having proved an empty dream, he was by no means without further reformative schemes. He and some admirers conceived the notion of the first of those periodicals which were to occupy so much of Coleridge's time and energy and bring in such small material rewards. In January 1796 he began a tour through the Midlands to the North to promote interest in *The Watchman*, a literary and political weekly. He also preached to Unitarian congregations at a number of places. He gained considerable attention, widespread esteem, and a promising list of subscribers. His letters describing this advertising tour are full of amusing episodes. A friend in Nottingham gave a prospectus of *The Watchman* to an aristocrat, who glanced at the motto: 'That all may know the truth, and that the truth may make us free', and remarked, 'A seditious beginning!' On being told that this motto was quoted from another author, the aristocrat said, 'What odds whether he wrote it himself or quoted it from any other seditious dog?' He was then told to look up the Gospel of St. John, Chapter VIII, verse 32, and he would find that the seditious dog was Jesus Christ.[1]

High spirits, however, alternated with periods of depression and self-reproach. News of Sara's ill-health at home in Bristol made him anxious to get back, and the tour was curtailed. In February he wrote to a friend: 'I am almost heartless! My past life seems to me like a dream, a feverish dream! all one gloomy huddle of strange actions, and dim-discovered motives! Friendships lost by indolence, and happiness murdered by mismanaged sensibility! the present hour I seem in a quickset-hedge of embarrassments! For shame! I ought not to mistrust God!'[2]

He suffered from periodical attacks of ill-health and sleeplessness, as a relief from which he had recourse to opium.

He returned to Bristol and immersed himself in preparations for the appearance of the first number of *The Watchman*. This was published the following month, and the publication continued for ten issues until it was finally discontinued in May 1796 because it failed to pay its expenses.

Meanwhile, with Joseph Cottle, the Bristol bookseller, he was arranging for the publication of a volume of his poems, of whose contents he regarded *Religious Musings* as the most

[1] Letter to John Edwards, 29th January 1796.
[2] Letter to Josiah Wade from Lichfield, February 1796.

xiv

important. Neither this nor any other of his projects brought him any relief from material worry. To Cottle he wrote in February 1796:

> The Future is cloud & thick darkness —— Poverty perhaps, and the thin faces of them that want bread looking up to me! —— Nor is this all —— my happiest moments for composition are broken in on by the reflection of —— I *must* make haste —— I am too late —— I am already months behind! I have received my *pay* beforehand! —— O way-ward and desultory Spirit of Genius! ill canst thou brook a task-master! The tenderest touch from the hand of *Obligation* wounds thee, like a scourge of Scorpions!

In May he accepted the generous offer by a Somerset friend, Thomas Poole, and a small group of admirers, of an annual payment of five guineas each, as a mark of their admiration. The total annuity amounted to £35 or £40,[1] and Coleridge was deeply touched by this genuinely philanthropic action, as well as to some extent relieved of financial worry. The payments continued until another benefactor offered Coleridge a far larger sum. The summer was spent in organizing a number of schemes for earning more money—journalism, lecturing, tutoring. A partial reconciliation with Southey was brought about. In September 1796 Coleridge's first child, Hartley, was born, and in December he moved with Sara and the baby to a cottage at Nether Stowey, in the Quantock Hills, south of Bristol, where they were neighbours of their friend and benefactor, Thomas Poole. To this period belongs Coleridge's self-portrait in a letter to the politician Thelwall:

> As to me, my face, unless when animated by immediate eloquence, expresses great Sloth, & great, indeed almost ideotic, good nature. 'Tis a mere carcase of a face: fat, flabby, & expressive chiefly of inexpression. —— Yet, I am told, that my eyes, eyebrows, & forehead are physiognomically good —— ; but of this the Deponent knoweth not. As to my shape, 'tis a good shape enough, if measured

[1] In present-day values, about £200.

—— but my gait is awkward, & the walk, & the *Whole man* indicates *indolence capable of energies.* —— I am, & ever have been, a great reader —— & have read almost every thing —— a library-cormorant —— I am *deep* in all out of the way books, whether of the monkish times, or of the puritanical era. . . . I seldom read except to amuse myself —— & I am almost always reading. —— Of useful knowledge, I am a so-so chemist, & I love chemistry —— all else is *blank,* —— but I *will* be (please God) an Horticulturist & a Farmer. I compose very little —— & I absolutely hate composition. Such is my dislike, that even a sense of Duty is sometimes too weak to overpower it.[1]

In March 1797 began that close association with William Wordsworth and his sister Dorothy which was one of the most important in Coleridge's life. The two men had first met in Bristol eighteen months before. Wordsworth and Dorothy settled at Alfoxden, only three miles away from Nether Stowey. The strength of the association that now began was due to its complementary character: Coleridge conceived an instant admiration for Wordsworth's achievement in poetry, for the naturalness and simplicity of its style in comparison with his own, which at this time was high-flown and florid. Wordsworth, as well as his sister, responded to the magnetism of Coleridge's personality, and the brilliance and fertility of his mind. Wordsworth was an indolent or indifferent reader, believing in the educative power of nature; Coleridge was omnivorous and insatiable, and deeply versed in ancient and modern learning. Coleridge perceived in Wordsworth those solid qualities of patience and tenacity of purpose which he himself lacked; Wordsworth found in Coleridge a foil to his own cautious and deliberate temperament.

The first of Coleridge's important poems written under the influence of Wordsworth's ideas was *This Lime-Tree Bower my Prison*, composed during the Wordsworths' first visit to Stowey with Charles Lamb. It is one of those expressions of the joy of

[1] Letters, 19th November 1796.

friendship which are among his best and most characteristic poems.

During the summer, owing to Coleridge's association with radical politicians such as Thelwall, he and Wordsworth became the object of the attentions of government spies. It was rumoured in the neighbourhood that sedition was being plotted at Alfoxden and Stowey, for this was the time when England was in the grip of the first invasion-scare. Wordsworth was already disillusioned with the hopes of world regeneration produced by the French Revolution in its opening phase, and Coleridge too lost interest in republicanism. Apart from poetry, his mind was continually occupied with philosophy and religion. He had by no means abandoned altogether the intention of earning a living as a Unitarian minister, and the material difficulties from which he still suffered, despite the generosity of friends, made him think once again of seeking some such employment. That winter, the approaching birth of a second child made some sort of material security imperative, and Coleridge went to Shrewsbury as candidate for a post as Unitarian minister. This was something of a crisis in his affairs. He made a very favourable impression on those who had invited him to consider the post, but he shrank from committing himself to a way of life which he knew would involve many irksome parochial duties and interfere with the free development of his intellectual and imaginative powers. Briefly, his sense of duty as a breadwinner was a strong inducement to accept the situation, while his instincts as poet made him draw back. He was on the point of accepting when the arrival of another offer proved decisive. Two brothers, Thomas and Josiah Wedgwood, of philanthropic temper and considerable wealth, offered Coleridge an annuity of £150 as a mark of their admiration and their confidence in his genius. The offer was unconditional and the annuity was to go on indefinitely, subject only to the continuance of the Wedgwoods' prosperity.

Coleridge was overcome by this munificence. He wrote at once to Josiah Wedgwood accepting the offer, and expressing his gratitude and admiration. He concluded: 'Disembarrassed from all pecuniary anxiety yet unshackled by any regular profession, with powerful motives & no less powerful propensities to honorable effort, it is my duty to indulge the hope that at some future period I shall have given a proof that as your intentions were eminently virtuous, so the action itself was not unbeneficent.'[1]

At this point it is worth while pausing to consider the comments of one of Coleridge's most distinguished biographers, Sir Edmund Chambers;[2] of his acceptance of the Wedgwood annuity, Chambers says:

> Perhaps the worst thing possible had happened to him. He had talked long enough; sown enough wild oats. I do not suggest that he should have become a Unitarian minister. But it was time for him, in one way or another, to take up his share of the economic burden which is, or ought to be, the common lot of humanity. Instead, here was an endowment which, in terms at least, left it possible to go on just as he had always done. It is true that his first impulse was to recognize in full the moral obligation which it imposed upon him. . . . But, unfortunately, the longer Coleridge looked at a moral obligation the more he became inclined in practice to shy away from it.

This is typical of the unsympathetic misunderstanding which has continued to dog Coleridge's memory for more than a century. Time and again his instincts as a creative writer made it impossible for him to accept regular employments. Nobody could have been more severely critical than he was of himself over his failure to meet obligations; but to entangle himself in such commitments was, to him, the supreme impossibility; it was a betrayal of those powers which he knew to be in him-

[1] Letters, 17th January, 1798.
[2] *Samuel Taylor Coleridge : A Biographical Study*. Oxford, 1938.

self, and which all men of judgement who knew him at this time believed in. 'To sow wild oats' is a strange expression to use of a young man who had married from a sense of moral obligation, and had been guilty of no worse dissipation than reading when he might have been writing for a living. If he was not to accept a post as Unitarian minister, what sort of employment do Coleridge's critics envisage for him? He said later that he could have earned £2000 a year by writing articles for the *Morning Post*. But he was not by nature a political journalist, though necessity made him engage deeply in such work. Failure of sympathetic understanding in Coleridge's case can only come from a fundamental lack of artistic sensibility. The Wedgwood annuity came at the beginning of what every critic of discernment has regarded as Coleridge's *annus mirabilis*. For the freedom from material anxiety, together with his new friendship with the Wordsworths and his comparative domestic calm combined to produce such a liberation of spirit, such a release of creative power, that the year 1798 became the year of Coleridge's greatest poetic achievement. And we are told that he ought to have taken a job!

We are told also that he was an incessant talker, as if that somehow were a needless luxury, a squandering of time which ought to have been spent on something more lucrative. That again is to betray a total misunderstanding of the essential oneness of human personality. If we value *The Ancient Mariner, Kubla Khan,* the fragment of *Christabel, Dejection, Frost at Midnight* and those other evidences of a unique genius, it is useless to deplore the conditions in which they were created. Most of his best poetry is based on a conviction of the importance of love. His whole life was centred in the need to give and to receive love. His vast philosophic and religious schemes arose from a love of humanity. But with Coleridge, this was not, as with so many, an abstraction. He loved people, and he needed to be loved in return. As he wrote later:

To be beloved is all I need,
And whom I love, I love indeed.[1]

This was literally true. Because he needed love and esteem, he talked. He talked perpetually, and was never without an audience. Talking was as much a part of love as love was of life, and of Coleridge's life his poetry was the essence.

In May 1798 his second son, Berkeley, was born, and in the same month the plan of *Lyrical Ballads* was formed between him and Wordsworth. *The Ancient Mariner* was completed, and Coleridge turned to *Christabel,* which also was to have appeared in *Lyrical Ballads.* But this poem was never finished. *Kubla Khan* has been variously dated 1797 and 1798. In October 1798 *Lyrical Ballads* appeared. It sold badly, and the critics were either indifferent or openly hostile. Wordsworth later ascribed its failure to the presence of *The Ancient Mariner.*

Meanwhile, the two poets, with Dorothy and another friend, went to Germany. They separated, and Coleridge became homesick and anxious about his children's welfare. In the spring of 1799 Berkeley died of a consumptive cough, but Coleridge remained in Germany collecting materials for a work he intended to write on German literature. By the end of July he was back at Stowey.

During the winter of 1799 to 1800 Coleridge wrote political articles for the *Morning Post,* but by the following spring he had tired of this pursuit. He disliked journalism, and engaged in it solely to provide for his family. At home things were not easy. Continued financial difficulty did nothing to sweeten Sara's never docile temper, and gradually the temperamental gulf between husband and wife widened. Coleridge craved sympathy, indulgence, understanding, and intellectual companionship. He found none of these in his wife. On the contrary, his continued close relations with the Wordsworths only increased her resentment. Theirs was a companionship which

[1] *The Pains of Sleep,* 1803

Sara could not share. Meanwhile, in October 1799, Coleridge had paid a visit to the farm at Sockburn where the Hutchinsons lived—Mary was soon to be Wordsworth's wife. There he met Mary's sister, another Sara, who instantly impressed him by her possession of all those qualities which his wife lacked. She had all he could wish for, except beauty. During the next few years their friendship deepened, their mutual dependence turned into love—a love which could never be fulfilled, although it became the central emotion of Coleridge's life. Sara Hutchinson was the object of the series of poems addressed to 'Asra' and culminating in the great 'Dejection Ode' of 1802.

In 1800 the Coleridges removed to Keswick in order to be near the Wordsworths, who had settled at Grasmere. In September Derwent Coleridge was born. The following year saw the republication of *Lyrical Ballads,* with the famous preface setting forth the two poets' ideas on the nature of poetry, but without Coleridge's *Christabel,* which had been intended for inclusion. He never got beyond the second book although five had been projected. The poem, with its marvellous opening and its suggestion of something sinister beneath the surface, is symbolic of Coleridge's life at this period. His fruitless love for Sara Hutchinson, his increasing ill-health due to the climate of the Lake District, and his acute domestic distress weighed on his spirits and depressed his poetic genius. He talked of going abroad for his health, but nothing was done. It began to be recognized by their friends that the incompatibility between husband and wife was making their lives intolerable. Coleridge wrote to his brother-in-law:[1]

> O Friend! I am sadly shattered. The least agitation brings on bowel complaints, & within the last week *twice* with an ugly symptom—namely—of sickness even to vomiting—& Sara—alas! we are not suited to each other. But the months of my absence I devote to *self*-discipline, & to the attempt to draw her nearer to me by a regular

[1] Letter to Southey, 21st October 1801.

development of all the sources of our unhappiness—then for another Trial, *fair* as I hold the love of good men dear to me—*patient,* as I myself love my own dear children. I will go believing that it will end happily—if not, if our mutual unsuitableness continues, and (as it assuredly will do, if it continue) increases & strengthens, why then, it is better for her & my children, that I should live apart than that she should be a Widow & they Orphans. Carefully have I *thought thro'* the subject of marriage & deeply am I convinced of its indissolubleness.—If I separate, I do it in the earnest desire to provide for her & them; that while I live, she may enjoy the comforts of life; & that when I die, something may have been accumulated that may secure her from degrading Dependence. When I least love her, then most do I feel anxiety for her peace, comfort & welfare. Is she not the mother of my children? And am I the man not to know & feel this?

Coleridge began to consider a separation, and a long struggle was waged over this. Sara's pride made it impossible for her to consent to such a humiliation, and Coleridge's deep and passionate love for his children made him equally reluctant. So the cancer of domestic misery corroded his whole existence. The 'sacred river' of his creative energy was poisoned at the source. He turned to abstract thought and metaphysical speculation as a substitute for poetry. He knew that poetry could not be written by a man spiritually dead, and he lacked the will to force his genius against the effects of emotional sterility. In the spring of 1802 he poured out his sufferings to Sara Hutchinson in a long verse letter which is among the most agonizing confessional poems in English. This he subsequently published, in a much censored form, as *Dejection: an Ode.*

Of Coleridge at this crucial period Chambers writes:[1]

It must have become apparent during the course of this chronicle that Coleridge's failure to make good was primarily due to a fundamental instability of character. He had dreamed of the permanent, but had lived wholly in the present, talking brilliantly and incessantly, and snatching at every will-o'-the-wisp interest which a vivid imagina-

[1] Chambers, *op. cit.*

tion suggested to him. He could not integrate his life, and when troubles, for which he was not wholly responsible, came upon him, he had no reserve of endurance to make head against them. His gift of introspection sometimes gave him a whisper of this. 'Sloth jaundic'd all,' he had once said of himself, and had bewailed his 'chance-started friendships'. It was not exactly sloth. His mind was always actively at work upon something, only it was generally the wrong thing. And 'chance-started friendships' were to serve him well throughout life. So Coleridge drifted to disaster.

Here the biographer is echoing what others said of Coleridge from the very beginning of his misfortunes. Southey, for instance, wrote:[1]

It vexes and grieves me to the heart, that when he is gone, as go he will, nobody will believe what a mind goes with him,—how infinitely and ten-thousand-thousand-fold the mightiest of his generation.

Now it is true that Coleridge himself spoke of his 'sloth' and of his lack of will-power. But Coleridge, as an auto-biographer, was always his own worst enemy. Out of a kind of self-depreciatory generosity he gave his critics handles for every kind of misunderstanding and under-estimation. He was, it must be remembered, in even the most conventional sense, a good man. He began by loving his wife and he always loved his children and grieved that he could not provide for them. But his failure to 'make good', in his biographer's phrase, came not so much from an inability to integrate his life as from the lack of a suitable centre about which to integrate it. 'If my wife loved me, and I my wife, half as well as we both love our children,' he had written to Southey, 'I should be the happiest man alive—but this is not—will not be!' And in a letter to William Godwin in January 1802, he speaks of himself as 'struggling with sore calamities, with bodily pain, & languor—with pecuniary Difficulties—& worse than all, with domestic Discord, & the heart-withering Conviction—that I could not

[1] Robert Southey, *Letters.*

be happy without my children, & could not but be miserable with the mother of them.'

To Coleridge domestic affection, a man's private hearth, was the very centre of life: to seek a new and more satisfying centre by abandoning his wife and finding another would have been the solution which many would have sought. His incapacity to make a clean break, bound up as it was with his convictions as an active Christian, though it robbed him of any chance of happiness, sprang not from his sloth, nor his lack of direction, but from his goodness. He was an acutely sick man, and his sickness was intimately connected with his proximity to his wife. Such a fact would be better understood by doctors to-day than it was in his time. In the end he and Sara did indeed separate, after a sincere effort at reconciliation about the time of the birth of their third child in 1802—a daughter also called Sara. But the separation gave Coleridge no happiness, for by this time he had become wholly dependent, emotionally, on Sara Hutchinson, and neither his views nor hers would have permitted a union.

The years from 1802 to 1816 were a time of growing misery and hopelessness, relieved by spells of comparatively successful work and by the projection of multifarious schemes for making money and fame by writing and lecturing. In 1804 Coleridge at last went abroad, and for two and a half years was in Malta as secretary to the Governor, Sir Alexander Ball, and later in Italy. He obtained some relief from ill-health but none from poverty. On his return he hesitated to go back to his wife, and for a time lived with the Wordsworths. A more or less formal separation from Sara was, after lengthy wrangling, effected. He moved to London and began a series of lectures, of which great hopes were entertained by his many friends and admirers; but through ill-health and continued recourse to opium and alcohol, he proved a disappointing lecturer. Everyone admitted his flashes of brilliance, and the depth of his imaginative understanding of literature, but lamented his inability to sustain an argument or marshal his ideas in an orderly progression.

In London he was acutely unhappy. About 1808 he passed his old love, Mary Evans, in the street; she was now married and, like him, unhappy. He drifted into increasing dependence on opium and drink. He became somewhat estranged from the Wordsworths. Nevertheless, he joined them and Sara Hutchinson at Grasmere, where he tried to break himself of the opium addiction, and improved temporarily in health. He planned his last great attempt at a journal to be called *The Friend,* which was intended to be a general review of the arts, travel, morality and religion, philosophy and politics. Sara Hutchinson was to be his helper, and she indeed it was, according to Dorothy Wordsworth, who inspired Coleridge to carry on with the project as long as he did. *The Friend* lasted from June 1809 to March 1810, when it failed for lack of funds. The effort to keep Coleridge at work had worn Sara out, and she departed from Grasmere to live in Wales. Thus ended, in futile separation, the love which for the past twelve years had given Coleridge his firmest centre of happiness, tragic and fitful though that happiness had been.

Then followed the break-up of his long friendship with the Wordsworths. The cause of the breach was an unfavourable report on Coleridge's habits which Wordsworth had given to a mutual friend, Basil Montagu, with whom Coleridge proposed to live in London. He regarded this report as the grossest possible betrayal. According to Montagu, Wordsworth had told him that Coleridge's intemperance made him unfit for residence in Montagu's house, and had made him a positive nuisance at Grasmere. Coleridge left Montagu's house and went to a hotel. For the next few years he drifted from lodging to lodging in London, seeing old friends, delivering more public lectures in order to raise funds, suffering from chronic ill-health, and becoming more and more addicted to opium.

Gloomy and hopeless though these years were, they were not without periods of relief. In 1812, through the agency of a benevolent friend, Henry Crabb Robinson, a reconciliation with the Wordsworths took place. It was more formal than actual, and the old spirit of friendship was never revived. In the same year Coleridge's play *Ossorio,* was successfully produced at Drury Lane; but a heavy blow to his financial circumstances fell when the Wedgwoods' annuity was reduced owing to the brothers' losses during the wars. Illness and opium-addiction made his friends fear that he might commit suicide, so desperate in spirit had he become. At length, early in 1816, he was persuaded to see a new physician, Dr. James Gillman of Highgate, who undertook to reduce his reliance on opium and supervise his health. Accordingly he took up his residence in the Gillmans' household, where he remained until his death in 1834.

The enlightened doctor and his kindly wife restored him to something like health and tranquillity of mind. The storms or life were over. Financial anxiety continued to be his worst trouble, but he lived to enjoy respect, even fame, and to carry on the work of writing down his ideas on a great variety of subjects, as well as collecting and editing his previous scattered writings.

This is not to say, however, that Coleridge's life declined into an autumnal calm. He was, after all, less than forty-four when he took up residence with the Gillmans, though it was said that by the age of thirty he had already looked like an old man. He still had to provide for his family, who were living in the Lake District with his brother-in-law, Southey. Coleridge was in renewed financial difficulties, which he tried to overcome by lecturing and publishing.

In 1816 he issued in one volume *Kubla Khan,* the fragment of *Christabel,* and *The Pains of Sleep.* He published *Kubla Khan* with a typical self-depreciatory note to the effect that he had been urged to do so by 'a poet of great and deserved celebrity'

(Byron). He described the poem as 'a psychological curiosity'. His family circle at Keswick laughed at his venturing to publish the 'fragment', and posterity has been inclined to write it off as a piece of inspired jabberwocky. In spite of Coleridge's apologetics, I think we must accept *Kubla Khan* as a complete whole, and one of the most wonderful poems in this or any other language. It is discussed at some length in the notes to this volume.

In the following year Coleridge published *Biographia Literaria*, a great but uneven book, a strange mixture of autobiography, literary criticism, and philosophical speculation. It was put together somewhat hurriedly, and in places the writing is turgid; but no other book contains more profound and penetrating statements of æsthetic belief; to some readers it is the foundation of the art or science of literary criticism. In the same year appeared his collected poems, under the title of *Sibylline Leaves*.

In 1820 he was shocked to hear that Hartley had lost his probationary fellowship at Oriel College, Oxford, on the grounds of general unsuitability. He was, in fact, unreliable on account of a weakness for drink. Coleridge intervened unsuccessfully on his behalf, and Hartley returned to the Lakes to earn a living by teaching. His father never saw him again. He did, however, see other members of his family in London from time to time, especially his only daughter, Sara.

In spite of disappointments and difficulties, his life at Highgate was not unhappy, and in the Gillmans' household the affectionate and even intimate atmosphere preserved him from the worst effects of despair and ill-health. In 1824 he was elected a fellow of the newly founded Royal Society of Literature. He went to parties and talked incessantly. His regular Thursday evenings at Highgate were attended by literary men and women, and young aspirants to fame were glad to visit him and listen to his ever-flowing eloquence.

In 1828 he went for a last visit to the Continent with Words-
worth and his daughter Dora, but soon his health finally broke
down; he once more had recourse to opium and for the greater
part of three years was confined to his room. On 25th July
1834 he died in a coma, the cause of his death being given as
enlargement of the heart. A few months later his lifelong
friend Charles Lamb also died, his death being hastened by
inconsolable grief at the loss of Coleridge. The following year
Wordsworth wrote his *Extempore Effusion upon the Death of
James Hogg,* in which he laments the passing of a number of
poets during the previous year or so; and he speaks of the grief
he has felt

> Since every mortal power of Coleridge
> Was frozen at its marvellous source;
> The rapt One, of the godlike forehead,
> The heaven-eyed creature sleeps in earth.

Southey, on the other hand, according to Tom Moore,[1] said
that Coleridge was 'lamented by few, and regretted by none'.

In 1828 Coleridge had been visited by the young Thomas
Carlyle, whose highly unflattering account contains the words:
'I reckon him a man of great and useless genius: a strange, not
at all a great man'. This is an ill-considered judgement, but
something of its spirit has haunted the memory of Coleridge
for more than a century after his death. His biographer, Sir
Edmund Chambers, for instance, comments as follows on his
death: 'So Coleridge passed, leaving a handful of golden poems,
an emptiness in the hearts of a few friends, and a will-o'-the-
wisp light for bemused thinkers'. Matthew Arnold wrote on
all the foremost poets of the Romantic period, but not on
Coleridge.[2] Superficial reviewers still write of his 'handful of
poems'—without perhaps stopping to ask whose hand could

---

[1] *Diary,* 20th February 1835.
[2] One of the most sympathetic nineteenth-century estimates of Coleridge was
written by Walter Pater in 1865, and his essay in *Appreciations* is still worth reading.

contain *The Ancient Mariner*, even if Coleridge had written nothing else. He has for more than a century been judged by the quantity of what he did not write, rather than the quality of what he did. It was, of course, Coleridge himself, abetted by contemporaries who were supposed to be his friends, who started the legend of the great procrastinator, the projector of immense works which were never finished. Certainly it was his misfortune to achieve his greatest single poetic triumph before he was twenty-six. It was this that enabled a late Victorian critic, Leslie Stephen, to write: 'Coleridge's poetic impulse died early; perhaps, as De Quincey says, it was killed by the opium; or as Coleridge said himself, that his afflictions had suspended what nature gave him at his birth,

His shaping spirit of imagination.'

But it is not true that his poetic impulse died early. As Stephen himself wrote, 'Coleridge was, above all, essentially and intrinsically a poet'. It is not clear, in this context, exactly what Stephen meant by 'a poet', if by that title is meant one whose essential impulse can die early. Coleridge was at all times a poet, and this volume will, I hope, show that flashes at least of poetic creation occurred throughout his life. To expect of a poet a consistent level of achievement throughout his life, both in quality and in quantity, is entirely to misconceive the nature of his being. There are, during a poet's life, overwhelming reasons for writing poems; and there are also prolonged periods during which there are overwhelming reasons for not writing poems. This does not mean that during these periods he thereby ceases to be a poet.

Some, such as Wordsworth or Tennyson or Browning, were at all times able to write poems when there was no overwhelming reason for doing so. They thereby wrote much dull and un-rewarding stuff. Without a compelling occasion Coleridge could not write poems, and turned to other things. He wrote lectures, sermons, political articles, metaphysical essays, theology, translations, literary criticism—and especially he wrote long letters to his friends and filled about sixty notebooks with observations of all kinds. The immensity of his actual output is only now beginning to be fully appreciated. All this unceasing intellectual activity—to say nothing of the incessant talk he lavished upon his admirers—was the by-product of his dominating passion, poetry.

The life and writings of a poet form a continuum which is more significant than any part of his work taken in isolation. *The Ancient Mariner* is one of the greatest imaginative achievements in all literature, and it is senseless to isolate it, along with a 'handful' of other poems, from the rest of Coleridge and say, 'What a pity he didn't write more like it!' His life, his letters, his notebooks and his miscellaneous prose writings are the reason why the greatest of the poems are as great as they are. It would be as futile to look at Everest and say, 'What a pity the rest of the Himalayas are not so high!' The foothills, the lesser peaks, the great mass of the whole range, are the reason why Everest is as high as it is.

To revert to Carlyle's phrase, 'a great and useless genius', we may ask, 'Can genius ever be useless—or, which is the same thing, can it ever be useful?' The justification for a great genius is his existence—or rather, his influence in the widest sense; for genius is inconceivable without influence of some sort. A man who wrote nothing, created nothing, and spoke to no one, could hardly be called a genius, whatever gifts he might have been given at birth. The influence of Coleridge on his own time—on what we call the Romantic Movement—was immense; his influence on the future is likely also to be immense, when the full scope of his thought has been realized. He had what J. S. Mill called 'one of the great seminal minds'—that is, his writing and thinking, especially as it influenced such men as Wordsworth, were of incalculable power in affecting the development of thought during and after his time. In many departments of thought Coleridge was, indeed, before his time—which is perhaps why some of his contemporaries considered him useless. But in literary criticism, and more especially in psychology, he was one of the most original writers of all time. Psychology consists essentially in the study of the mind by the mind, and this was Coleridge's lifelong preoccupation. Reading his criticism—the lectures on Shakespeare, for instance—we are continually aware of his restless search into the mind of the creative artist, the imaginative insight with which he read a play or analyzed a poem. To a modern reader the literary criticism of the generation before Coleridge, the generation of Dr. Johnson, must always appear, despite its sterling qualities, comparatively superficial. Coleridge was the great germinating spirit of English Romanticism. It is impossible to doubt that, in the intimacy between him and Wordsworth which produced *Lyrical Ballads,* and the Preface to the second edition, it was he who was the guiding intelligence, the leading force. Much of the credit for Coleridge's seminal ideas went to Wordsworth, and this was another reason for the under-estimation of Coleridge by the nineteenth century. It was above all in the mind and writings of Coleridge that the various strands of the romantic idea which lay loose and scattered in eighteenth-century literature came together and formed the pattern by which the literature of the subsequent age is recognizable. *The Ancient Mariner* is a voyage of discovery in the limitless world of the imagination which had been hinted at in the 'Gothic' writings of the eighteenth century; it was a rediscovery of the world of the ancient ballads in terms of a contemporary conscience and consciousness: the Mariner, with his burden of guilt, is modern man forced to explore the lonely expanses of his own soul. The poem was not only a great imaginative achievement, utterly unlike anything that had been, or could have been, written before, it was a work of prophecy, a spiritual autobiography which the poet himself was forced to live out in the agony of his years of frustration. That Coleridge himself came to look upon his masterpiece in this light is shown by the reference to it in the Epitaph upon himself written a year or two before his death (see p. 127).

In *Christabel* he attempted once again to recapture the magic and suggestiveness of Gothic imagery, of the medieval spirit, which had been discarded by post-Elizabethan rationalism; fragmentary as it was, its influence was considerable: we have only to think of the poems of Keats and of the Pre-Raphaelites to realize the potentialities opened up by Coleridge's tale.

Of even greater influence, however, was the distinctive style of that series of introspective meditations which includes *This Lime-tree Bower my Prison, Frost at Midnight, Dejection* and *Youth and Age,* and which was to some extent foreshadowed in *The Eolian Harp* and other early works.

As early as 1794 Coleridge had shown his interest in the poems of Akenside, a somewhat neglected eighteenth-century precursor of romanticism, by writing an elegy in imitation of him. Akenside was a writer of descriptive blank verse which at its best could easily be mistaken for the characteristic blank verse of Wordsworth. But while Akenside, and to some extent Wordsworth, meditated *on* nature, and expressed their feelings in a context of natural description, it was Coleridge's peculiar contribution to introspective, autobiographical poetry to fuse external description and inner feeling in a way never achieved before. The 'scenery' of *Frost at Midnight* and *Dejection,* in a sense, *is* the emotion of these poems; feeling and description are one. This is the origin of modern introspective nature poetry.

In the Renaissance and the early seventeenth century the relation between man and nature was a symbolic one. Man was the apex of an ordered hierarchy in which plants and animals had their appointed places, and derived their significance from their relation to man. This significance was lost in the scientific rational era which followed. The early Romantics attempted to re-discover external nature by making it the scene, the context, of man's reflections. It was the triumph of the Lake poets, and notably Coleridge, to re-integrate man and nature, not indeed in a symbolic relationship (flowers and animals did not 'stand for' this or that human attribute—the rose for passion, the lion for kingliness, and so on) but in a psychological one. Mountains, lakes, the moon, the colours of the sky, streams and woods discovered afresh by personal exploration and precise observation (of which Dorothy Wordsworth's journals and Coleridge's notebooks are the eloquent witness) became identified with childhood influences, states of feeling, all the varying moods to which poets were subject. This view of nature later caused Ruskin to describe the attribution of human feelings to so-called inanimate nature as the 'pathetic fallacy': but to the Romantics it was not a fallacy but a faith.

All the major Romantics, from Blake to Clare, were engaged, in their different ways, in the re-discovery of nature, the assertion of the one-ness of man and the rest of creation. It was their way of salvation from the dangerous sterility of eighteenth-century scientific rationalism. One of Coleridge's 'seminal' remarks is a brief comment to be found in one of his notebooks: 'Poetry without egotism comparatively uninteresting.' That is to say, poetry concerned with the description of external nature, or with merely objective themes, did not interest him. The true subject of poetry was, in his view, the human ego, the psyche, the soul of man in isolation. His story is a heroic one, not in any obvious sense, but because it reveals a man living for and by his feelings—above all, the feeling of love, by which we are bound, for good or ill, to the rest of the human kind. He had the courage of his egotism, though being a sincerely religious man, he was essentially humble. Most men attempt to escape from their feelings by taking refuge in social activities, a conventional occupation, or in trivialities of one sort or another. ('Better to do nothing than nothings', Coleridge wrote.) As it is the business of the painter to see, and the business of the philosopher to reason, so, to Coleridge, it is the business of the poet to feel. He was not the man to give way to a histrionic or a selfish indulgence of feeling, like Byron or Shelley; but he felt impelled by inner necessity to remain alive and sensitive to feeling, whatever it cost him. Coleridge's Mariner was a man who had violated the principle of love, of regard for natural creation, by killing the albatross; his greatness consists in his having accepted the full responsibility for his action and undergone the extremes of penance.

> Alone, alone, all, all alone,
>   Alone on a wide wide sea!
> And never a saint took pity on
>   My soul in agony.

Regeneration comes with the re-discovery of the love of creation. But only a soul which has suffered as the Mariner suffered could fully know and realize all its wonder and beauty. The astonishing and inexplicable thing about Coleridge's poetry is that he should have written his masterpiece so early, that he should have experienced life so profoundly at a subconscious level before he proved the experiences behind the poem in his own life. For there is evidence that during the period of its composition he was at his happiest. Almost the whole of the rest of his life was spent in discovering and undergoing the agony of spirit he had so movingly *pre*-experienced, as it were, in imagination.

Unlike some of the poems and many of the letters, the notebooks of Coleridge, now in the course of publication, do not reveal an unhappy man. Rather, they reveal a mind infinitely receptive, a sensibility perpetually eager for new impressions and experiences, a restless and enquiring intelligence, a spirit incapable of boredom, a heart never weary or afraid of emotion, however painful, and it may be added, a lover of gaiety and humour. For this receptivity, this freshness and largeness of spirit, he paid a high price. Yet in remaining what he was to the end of his life, neither hardened nor embittered nor withered to insensibility, he triumphed. 'Call him Coleridge; I hate *poor* as applied to such a man. I can't bear to hear such a man pitied.' Lamb was right.

SELECTED POEMS

COLLECTED POEMS

Sonnet

Mild Splendour of the various-vested Night!
Mother of wildly-working visions! hail!
I watch thy gliding, while with watery light
Thy weak eye glimmers through a fleecy veil;
And when thou lovest thy pale orb to shroud   5
Behind the gathered blackness lost on high;
And when thou dartest from the wind-rent cloud
Thy placid lightning o'er the awakened sky.
Ah such is Hope! as changeful and as fair!
Now dimly peering on the wistful sight;   10
Now hid behind the dragon-winged Despair:
But soon emerging in her radiant might
She o'er the sorrow-clouded breast of Care
Sails, like a meteor kindling in its flight.

Destruction of the Bastille

I

Heard'st thou yon universal cry,
    And dost thou linger still on Gallia's shore?
Go, Tyranny! beneath some barbarous sky
    Thy terrors lost, and ruin'd power deplore!

I

What tho' through many a groaning age   5
Was felt thy keen suspicious rage,
Yet Freedom rous'd by fierce Disdain
Has wildly broke thy triple chain,
And like the storm which earth's deep entrails hide,
At length has burst its way and spread the ruins wide.   10

*   *   *   *   *

IV

In sighs their sickly breath was spent; each gleam
   Of Hope had ceas'd the long long day to cheer;
Or if delusive, in some flitting dream,
   It gave them to their friends and children dear—
      Awak'd by lordly Insult's sound   15
      To all the doubled horrors round,
      Oft shrunk they from Oppression's band
      While anguish rais'd the desperate hand
For silent death; or lost the mind's control,
Thro' every burning vein would tides of Frenzy roll.   20

V

But cease, ye pitying bosoms, cease to bleed!
   Such scenes no more demand the tear humane;
I see, I see! glad Liberty succeed
   With every patriot virtue in her train!
      And mark yon peasant's raptured eyes;   25
      Secure he views his harvests rise;
      No fetter vile the mind shall know,
      And Eloquence shall fearless glow.
Yes! Liberty the soul of Life shall reign,
Shall throb in every pulse, shall flow thro' every vein!   30

2

VI

Shall France alone a Despot spurn?
  Shall she alone, O Freedom, boast thy care?
Lo, round thy standard Belgia's heroes burn,
  Tho' Power's blood-stain'd streamers fire the air,
    And wider yet thy influence spread,   35
    Nor e'er recline thy weary head,
    Till every land from pole to pole
    Shall boast one independent soul!
And still, as erst, let favor'd Britain be
First ever of the first and freest of the free!   40

Monody on the Death of Chatterton

    Cold penury repress'd his noble rage,
    And froze the genial current of his soul.

  Now prompts the Muse poetic lays,
    And high my bosom beats with love of Praise!
  But, Chatterton! methinks I hear thy name,
For cold my Fancy grows, and dead each Hope of Fame.
    When Want and cold Neglect had chill'd thy soul,   5
Athirst for Death I see thee drench the bowl!
    Thy corpse of many a livid hue
    On the bare ground I view,
  Whilst various passions all my mind engage;
    Now is my breast distended with a sigh,   10
    And now a flash of Rage
Darts through the tear, that glistens in my eye.

  Is this the land of liberal Hearts!
  Is this the land, where Genius ne'er in vain
Pour'd forth her soul-enchanting strain?   15

Ah me! yet Butler 'gainst the bigot foe
   Well-skill'd to aim keen Humour's dart,
   Yet Butler felt Want's poignant sting;
    And Otway, Master of the Tragic art,
    Whom Pity's self had taught to sing,   20
   Sank beneath a load of Woe;
 This ever can the generous Briton hear,
And starts not in his eye th' indignant Tear?

   Elate of Heart and confident of Fame,
From vales where Avon sports, the Minstrel came,   25
   Gay as the Poet hastes along
   He meditates the future song,
How Ælla battled with his country's foes,
  And whilst Fancy in the air
  Paints him many a vision fair   30
His eyes dance rapture and his bosom glows.
With generous joy he views th' ideal gold:
  He listens to many a Widow's prayers,
  And many an Orphan's thanks he hears;
   He soothes to peace the care-worn breast,   35
   He bids the Debtor's eyes know rest,
   And Liberty and Bliss behold:
And now he punishes the heart of steel,
And her own iron rod he makes Oppression feel.

Fated to heave sad Disappointment's sigh,   40
To feel the Hope now rais'd, and now deprest,
To feel the burnings of an injur'd breast,
  From all thy Fate's deep sorrow keen
  In vain, O Youth, I turn th' affrighted eye;
  For powerful Fancy evernigh   45
The hateful picture forces on my sight.
  There, Death of every dear delight,

Frowns Poverty of Giant mien!
In vain I seek the charms of youthful grace,
Thy sunken eye, thy haggard cheeks it shews,   50
The quick emotions struggling in the Face
    Faint index of thy mental Throes,
When each strong Passion spurn'd controll,
And not a Friend was nigh to calm thy stormy soul.

Such was the sad and gloomy hour   55
When anguish'd Care of sullen brow
Prepared the Poison's death-cold power.
Already to thy lips was rais'd the bowl,
When filial Pity stood thee by,
Thy fixéd eyes she bade thee roll   60
On scenes that well might melt thy soul—
Thy native cot she held to view,
Thy native cot, where Peace ere long
Had listen'd to thy evening song;
Thy sister's shrieks she bade thee hear,   65
And mark thy mother's thrilling tear,
She made thee feel her deep-drawn sigh,
And all her silent agony of Woe.

And from *thy* Fate shall such distress ensue?
Ah! dash the poison'd chalice from thy hand!   70
And thou had'st dash'd it at her soft command;
But that Despair and Indignation rose,
And told again the story of thy Woes,
Told the keen insult of th' unfeeling Heart,
The dread dependence on the low-born mind,   75
Told every Woe, for which thy breast might smart,
Neglect and grinning scorn and Want combin'd—
    Recoiling back, thou sent'st the friend of Pain
To roll a tide of Death thro' every freezing vein.

5

O Spirit blest!
Whether th' eternal Throne around,
Amidst the blaze of Cherubim,
Thou pourest forth the grateful hymn,
Or, soaring through the blest Domain,
Enraptur'st Angels with thy strain,— 85
Grant me, like thee, the lyre to sound,
Like thee, with fire divine to glow—
But ah! when rage the Waves of Woe,
Grant me with firmer breast t'oppose their hate,
And soar beyond the storms with upright eye elate! 90

Pain

Once could the Morn's first beams, the healthful breeze,
All nature charm, and gay was every hour:—
But ah! not Music's self, nor fragrant bower
Can glad the trembling sense of wan disease.
Now that the frequent pangs my frame assail, 5
Now that my sleepless eyes are sunk and dim,
And seas of pain seem waving through each limb—
Ah what can all Life's gilded scenes avail?
I view the crowd, whom youth and health inspire,
Hear the loud laugh, and catch the sportive lay, 10
Then sigh and think—I too could laugh and play
And gaily sport it on the Muse's lyre,
Ere Tyrant Pain had chas'd away delight,
Ere the wild pulse throbb'd anguish thro' the night!

Genevieve

Maid of my Love, sweet Genevieve!
In Beauty's light you glide along:
Your eye is like the star of eve,
And sweet your Voice, as Seraph's song.
Yet not your heavenly Beauty gives   5
This heart with passion soft to glow:
Within your soul a Voice there lives!
It bids you hear the tale of Woe.
When sinking low the Sufferer wan
Beholds no hand outstretcht to save,   10
Fair, as the bosom of the Swan
That rises graceful o'er the wave,
I've seen your breast with pity heave,
And therefore love I you, sweet Genevieve!

Inside the Coach

'Tis hard on Bagshot Heath to try
   Unclos'd to keep the weary eye;
But ah! Oblivion's nod to get
   In rattling coach is harder yet.
Slumbrous God of half shut eye!   5
   Who lov'st with Limbs supine to lie;
Soother sweet of toil and care
   Listen, listen to my prayer;
And to thy votary dispense
   Thy soporific influence!   10

What tho' around thy drowsy head
   The seven-fold cap of night be spread,
Yet lift that drowsy head awhile
   And yawn propitiously a smile;
In drizzly rains poppean dews   15
   O'er the tir'd inmates of the Coach diffuse;
And when thou'st charm'd our eyes to rest
   Pillowing the chin upon the breast,
Bid many a dream from thy dominions
   Wave its various-painted pinions,   20
Till ere the splendid visions close
     We snore quartettes in extacy of nose.
     While thus we urge our airy course,
     Oh may no jolt's electric force
     Our fancies from their steeds unhorse,   25
And call us from thy fairy reign
To dreary Bagshot Heath again!

A Wish

WRITTEN IN JESUS WOOD, FEB. 10, 1792

Lo! through the dusky silence of the groves,
Thro' vales irriguous, and thro' green retreats,
With languid murmur creeps the placid stream
       And works its secret way.

Awhile meand'ring round its native fields   5
It rolls the playful wave and winds its flight:
Then downward flowing with awaken'd speed
       Embosoms in the Deep!

Thus thro' its silent tenor may my Life
Smooth its meek stream by sordid wealth unclogg'd,   10
Alike unconscious of forensic storms,
      And Glory's blood-stain'd palm!

And when dark Age shall close Life's little day,
Satiate of sport, and weary of its toils,
E'en thus may slumbrous Death my decent limbs   15
      Compose with icy hand!

Sonnet

TO THE RIVER OTTER

Dear native brook! wild streamlet of the West!
  How many various-fated years have past,
  What happy, and what mournful hours, since last
I skimmed the smooth thin stone along thy breast,
Numbering its light leaps! yet so deep imprest   5
Sink the sweet scenes of childhood, that mine eyes
  I never shut amid the sunny ray,
But straight with all their tints thy waters rise,
  Thy crossing plank, thy marge with willows grey,
And bedded sand that, veined with various dyes,   10
Gleamed through thy bright transparence! On my way,
  Visions of childhood! oft have ye beguiled
Lone manhood's cares, yet waking fondest sighs:
  Ah! that once more I were a careless child!

The Sigh

When Youth his faery reign began
Ere sorrow had proclaimed me man;
While Peace the present hour beguiled,
And all the lovely Prospect smiled;
Then Mary! 'mid my lightsome glee   5
I heav'd the painless Sigh for thee.

And when, along the waves of woe,
My harassed Heart was doomed to know
The frantic burst of Outrage keen,
And the slow Pang that gnaws unseen;   10
Then shipwrecked on Life's stormy sea
I heaved an anguished Sigh for thee!

But soon Reflection's power imprest
A stiller sadness on my breast;
And sickly hope with waning eye   15
Was well content to droop and die:
I yielded to the stern decree,
Yet heaved a languid Sigh for thee!

And though in distant climes to roam,
A wanderer from my native home,   20
I fain would soothe the sense of Care,
And lull to sleep the Joys that were,
Thy Image may not banished be—
Still, Mary! still I sigh for thee.

Pantisocracy

No more my visionary soul shall dwell
On joys that were; no more endure to weigh
The shame and anguish of the evil day,
Wisely forgetful! O'er the ocean swell
Sublime of Hope, I seek the cottag'd dell   5
Where Virtue calm with careless step may stray,
And dancing to the moonlight roundelay,
The wizard Passions weave an holy spell.
Eyes that have ach'd with Sorrow! Ye shall weep
Tears of doubt-mingled joy, like theirs who start   10
From Precipices of distemper'd sleep,
On which the fierce-eyed Fiends their revels keep,
And see the rising Sun, and feel it dart
New rays of pleasance trembling to the heart.

On a Discovery made Too Late

Thou bleedest, my poor Heart! and thy distress
Reasoning I ponder with a scornful smile,
And probe thy sore wound sternly, though the while
Swoln be mine eye and dim with heaviness.
Why didst thou listen to Hope's whisper bland?   5
Or, listening, why forget the healing tale,
When Jealousy with feverous fancies pale
Jarred thy fine fibres with a maniac's hand?
Faint was that Hope, and rayless!—Yet 'twas fair,
And soothed with many a dream the hour of rest: 10

11

Thou shouldst have loved it most, when most opprest,
And nursed it with an agony of care,
Even as a Mother her sweet infant heir
That wan and sickly droops upon her breast!

Melancholy

A FRAGMENT

Stretch'd on a mouldered Abbey's broadest wall,
   Where ruining ivies propped the ruins steep—
Her folded arms wrapping her tattered pall,
   Had melancholy mus'd herself to sleep.
     The fern was press'd beneath her hair,   5
     The dark green adder's tongue was there;
And still as past the flagging sea-gale weak,
The long lank leaf bowed fluttering o'er her cheek.

That pallid cheek was flushed: her eager look
   Beamed eloquent in slumber! Inly wrought,   10
     Imperfect sounds her moving lips forsook,
   And her bent forehead worked with troubled thought.
     Strange was the dream—

To a Young Ass

Poor little Foal of an oppressed Race!
I love the languid Patience of thy face:
And oft with gentle hand I give thee bread,
And clap thy ragged Coat, and pat thy head.
But what thy dulled Spirits hath dismayed,   5
That never thou dost sport along the glade?
And (most unlike the nature of things young)
That earthward still thy moveless head is hung?
Do thy prophetic Fears anticipate,
Meek Child of Misery! thy future fate?   10
The starving meal, and all the thousand aches
'Which patient Merit of the Unworthy takes?'
Or is thy sad heart thrilled with filial pain
To see thy wretched Mother's shortened Chain?
And, truly very piteous is her Lot—   15
Chained to a Log within a narrow spot,
Where the close-eaten Grass is scarcely seen,
While sweet around her waves the tempting Green!
Poor Ass! thy master should have learnt to show
Pity—best taught by fellowship of Woe!   20
For much I fear me that He lives like thee,
Half famished in a land of Luxury!
How askingly its footsteps hither bend,
It seems to say, 'And have I then one Friend?'
Innocent Foal! thou poor despised Forlorn!   25
I hail thee Brother—spite of the fool's scorn!

And fain would take thee with me, in the Dell
Of Peace and mild Equality to dwell,
Where Toil shall call the charmer Health his bride,
And Laughter tickle Plenty's ribless side!　　　　　30
How thou wouldst toss thy heels in gamesome play,
And frisk about, as lamb or kitten gay!
Yea! and more musically sweet to me
Thy dissonant harsh bray of joy would be,
Than warbled melodies that soothe to rest　　　　　35
The aching of pale Fashion's vacant breast!

To the Nightingale

Sister of love-lorn Poets, Philomel!
How many Bards in city garret pent,
While at their window they with downward eye
Mark the faint lamp-beam on the kennell'd mud,
And listen to the drowsy cry of Watchmen　　　　　5
(Those hoarse unfeather'd Nightingales of Time!),
How many wretched Bards address *thy* name,
And hers, the full-orb'd Queen that shines above.
But I *do* hear thee, and the high bough mark,
Within whose mild moon-mellow'd foliage hid　　　　　10
Thou warblest sad thy pity-pleading strains.
O! I have listen'd, till my working soul,
Waked by those strains to thousand phantasies,
Absorb'd hath ceas'd to listen! Therefore oft,
I hymn thy name: and with a proud delight　　　　　15
Oft will I tell thee, Minstrel of the Moon!
'Most musical, most melancholy' Bird!
That all thy soft diversities of tone,
Tho' sweeter far than the delicious airs

That vibrate from a white-arm'd Lady's harp,   20
What time the languishment of lonely love
Melts in her eye, and heaves her breast of snow,
Are not so sweet as is the voice of her,
My Sara—best beloved of human kind!
When breathing the pure soul of tenderness,   25
She thrills me with the Husband's promis'd name!

Lines

COMPOSED WHILE CLIMBING THE LEFT ASCENT OF
BROCKLEY COOMB, SOMERSETSHIRE, MAY, 1795

With many a pause and oft reverted eye
I climb the Coomb's ascent: sweet songsters near
Warble in shade their wild-wood melody:
Far off the unvarying Cuckoo soothes my ear.
Up scour the startling stragglers of the Flock   5
That on green plots o'er precipices browse:
From the deep fissures of the naked rock
The Yew tree bursts! Beneath its dark green boughs
(Mid which the May-thorn blends its blossoms white)
Where broad smooth stones jut out in mossy seats,   10
I rest:—and now have gained the topmost site.
Ah! what a luxury of landscape meets
My gaze! Proud towers, and cots more dear to me,
Elm-shadow'd fields, and prospect-bounding sea!
Deep sighs my lonely heart: I drop the tear: 15
Enchanting spot! O were my Sara here!

The Eolian Harp

My pensive Sara! thy soft cheek reclined
Thus on mine arm, most soothing sweet it is
To sit beside our cot, our cot o'ergrown
With white-flowered jasmin, and the broad-leaved myrtle,
(Meet emblems they of Innocence and Love!)   5
And watch the clouds, that late were rich with light,
Slow saddening round, and mark the star of eve
Serenely brilliant (such should wisdom be)
Shine opposite! How exquisite the scents
Snatched from yon bean-field! and the world so hushed!   10
The stilly murmur of the distant sea
Tells us of silence.
              And that simplest lute,
Placed length-ways in the clasping casement, hark!
How by the desultory breeze caressed,
Like some coy maid half yielding to her lover,   15
It pours such sweet upbraiding, as must needs
Tempt to repeat the wrong! And now, its strings
Boldlier swept, the long sequacious notes
Over delicious surges sink and rise,
Such a soft floating witchery of sound   20
As twilight Elfins make, when they at eve
Voyage on gentle gales from Fairy-Land,
Where Melodies round honey-dropping flowers,
Footless and wild, like birds of Paradise,
Nor pause, nor perch, hovering on untamed wing!   25
O the one life within us and abroad,

Which meets all motion and becomes its soul,
A light in sound, a sound-like power in light
Rhythm in all thought, and joyance every where—
Methinks, it should have been impossible   30
Not to love all things in a world so filled;
Where the breeze warbles, and the mute still air
Is Music slumbering on her instrument.

And thus, my love! as on the midway slope
Of yonder hill I stretch my limbs at noon,   35
Whilst through my half-closed eye-lids I behold
The sunbeams dance, like diamonds, on the main,
And tranquil muse upon tranquillity;
Full many a thought uncalled and undetained,
And many idle flitting phantasies,   40
Traverse my indolent and passive brain,
As wild and various as the random gales
That swell and flutter on this subject lute!
    And what if all of animated nature
Be but organic harps diversely framed,   45
That tremble into thought, as o'er them sweeps
Plastic and vast, one intellectual breeze,
At once the Soul of each, and God of All?
    But thy more serious eye a mild reproof
Darts, O beloved woman! nor such thoughts   50
Dim and unhallowed dost thou not reject,
And biddest me walk humbly with my God.
Meek daughter in the family of Christ!
Well hast thou said and holily dispraised
These shapings of the unregenerate mind;   55
Bubbles that glitter as they rise and break
On vain Philosophy's aye-babbling spring.
For never guiltless may I speak of him,
The Incomprehensible! save when with awe

I praise him, and with Faith that inly feels;   **60**
Who with his saving mercies healed me,
A sinful and most miserable man,
Wildered and dark, and gave me to possess
Peace, and this cot, and thee, heart-honoured Maid!

This Lime-Tree Bower my Prison

In the June of 1797, some long-expected Friends paid a visit to the author's cottage; and on the morning of their arrival, he met with an accident, which disabled him from walking during the whole time of their stay. One evening, when they had left him for a few hours, he composed the following lines in the garden-bower.

Well, they are gone, and here must I remain,
This lime-tree bower my prison! I have lost
Beauties and feelings, such as would have been
Most sweet to my remembrance even when age
Had dimmed mine eyes to blindness! They, meanwhile,   5
Friends, whom I never more may meet again,
On springy heath, along the hill-top edge,
Wander in gladness, and wind down, perchance,
To that still roaring dell, of which I told;
The roaring dell, o'erwooded, narrow, deep,   10
And only speckled by the mid-day sun;
Where its slim trunk the ash from rock to rock
Flings arching like a bridge;—that branchless ash,
Unsunned and damp, whose few poor yellow leaves
Ne'er tremble in the gale, yet tremble still,   15
Fanned by the water-fall! and there my friends
Behold the dark green file of long lank weeds,
That all at once (a most fantastic sight!)

Still nod and drip beneath the dripping edge
Of the blue clay-stone.

                    Now, my friends emerge   20
Beneath the wide wide Heaven—and view again
The many-steepled tract magnificent
Of hilly fields and meadows, and the sea,
With some fair bark, perhaps, whose sails light up
The slip of smooth clear blue betwixt two Isles   25
Of purple shadow! Yes! they wander on
In gladness all; but thou, methinks, most glad,
My gentle-hearted Charles! for thou hast pined
And hungered after Nature, many a year,
In the great City pent, winning thy way   30
With sad yet patient soul, through evil and pain
And strange calamity! Ah! slowly sink
Behind the western ridge, thou glorious sun!
Shine in the slant beams of the sinking orb,
Ye purple heath-flowers! richlier burn, ye clouds!   35
Live in the yellow light, ye distant groves!
And kindle, thou blue ocean! So my Friend
Struck with deep joy may stand, as I have stood,
Silent with swimming sense; yea, gazing round
On the wide landscape, gaze till all doth seem   40
Less gross than bodily; and of such hues
As veil the Almighty Spirit, when yet he makes
Spirits perceive his presence.
                    A delight
Comes sudden on my heart, and I am glad
As I myself were there! Nor in this bower,   45
This little lime-tree bower, have I not marked
Much that has soothed me. Pale beneath the blaze
Hung the transparent foliage; and I watched
Some broad and sunny leaf, and loved to see

The shadow of the leaf and stem above 50
Dappling its sunshine! And that walnut-tree
Was richly tinged, and a deep radiance lay
Full on the ancient ivy, which usurps
Those fronting elms, and now, with blackest mass
Makes their dark branches gleam a lighter hue 55
Through the late twilight: and though now the bat
Wheels silent by, and not a swallow twitters,
Yet still the solitary humble bee
Sings in the bean-flower! Henceforth I shall know
That Nature ne'er deserts the wise and pure; 60
No plot so narrow, be but Nature there,
No waste so vacant, but may well employ
Each faculty of sense, and keep the heart
Awake to Love and Beauty! and sometimes
'Tis well to be bereft of promised good, 65
That we may lift the Soul, and contemplate
With lively joy the joys we cannot share.
My gentle-hearted Charles! when the last rook
Beat its straight path along the dusky air
Homewards, I blest it! deeming, its black wing 70
(Now a dim speck, now vanishing in light)
Had crossed the mighty orb's dilated glory,
While thou stood'st gazing; or when all was still,
¹ Flew creeking o'er thy head, and had a charm
For thee, my gentle-hearted Charles, to whom 75
No sound is dissonant which tells of Life.

¹ *Flew creeking*.] Some months after I had written this line, it gave me pleasure
to find that Bartram had observed the same circumstance of the Savanna Crane.
'When these Birds move their wings in flight, their strokes are slow, moderate
and regular; and even when at a considerable distance or high above us, we
plainly hear the quill-feathers; their shafts and webs upon one another creek as
the joints or working of a vessel in a tempestuous sea.'

The Rime of the Ancient Mariner

IN SEVEN PARTS

FACILE credo, plures esse Naturas invisibiles quam visibiles in rerum universitate. Sed horum omnium familiam quis nobis enarrabit, et gradus et cognationes et discrimina et singulorum munera? Quid agunt? quæ loca habitant? Harum rerum notitiam semper ambivit ingenium humanum, nunquam attigit. Juvat, interea, non diffiteor, quandoque in animo, tanquam in tabulâ, majoris et melioris mundi imaginem contemplari: ne mens assuefactâ hodiernæ vitæ minutiis se contrahat nimis, et tota subsidat in pusillas cogitationes. Sed veritati interea invigilandum est, modusque servandus, ut certa ab incertis, diem a nocte, distinguamus.

T. BURNET. ARCHÆOL. PHIL. p. 68.

PART I

It is an ancient Mariner,
And he stoppeth one of three.
'By thy long grey beard and glittering eye,
Now wherefore stopp'st thou me?

An ancient Mariner meeteth three gallants bidden to a wedding-feast, and detaineth one.

'The Bridegroom's doors are opened wide,
And I am next of kin;
The guests are met, the feast is set:
May'st hear the merry din.'

He holds him with his skinny hand,
'There was a ship,' quoth he.
'Hold off! unhand me, grey-beard loon!'
Eftsoons his hand dropt he.

21

The wedding guest is spell-bound by the eye of the old sea-faring man, and constrained to hear his tale.

He holds him with his glittering eye—
The wedding-guest stood still,
And listens like a three years' child:
The Mariner hath his will.

The wedding-guest sat on a stone:
He cannot choose but hear;
And thus spake on that ancient man,
The bright-eyed Mariner.

The ship was cheered, the harbour cleared,
Merrily did we drop
Below the kirk, below the hill,
Below the light house top.

The Mariner tells how the ship sailed southward with a good wind and fair weather, till it reached the Line.

The sun came up upon the left,
Out of the sea came he!
And he shone bright, and on the right
Went down into the sea.

Higher and higher every day,
Till over the mast at noon—
The Wedding-Guest here beat his breast,
For he heard the loud bassoon.

The wedding guest heareth the bridal music; but the Mariner continueth his tale.

The bride hath paced into the hall,
Red as a rose is she;
Nodding their heads before her goes
The merry minstrelsy.

The Wedding-Guest he beat his breast,
Yet he cannot choose but hear;
And thus spake on that ancient man,
The bright-eyed Mariner.

And now the storm-blast came, and he
Was tyrannous and strong:
He struck with his o'ertaking wings,
And chased us south along.

The ship drawn by a storm toward the south pole.

With sloping masts and dipping prow,
As who pursued with yell and blow
Still treads the shadow of his foe,
And forward bends his head,
The ship drove fast, loud roared the blast,
And southward aye we fled.

And now there came both mist and snow,
And it grew wondrous cold:
And ice, mast-high, came floating by,
As green as emerald.

And through the drifts the snowy clifts
Did send a dismal sheen:
Nor shapes of men nor beasts we ken—
The ice was all between.

The land of ice, and of fearful sounds where no living thing was to be seen.

The ice was here, the ice was there,
The ice was all around:
It cracked and growled, and roared and howled,
Like noises in a swound!

At length did cross an Albatross,
Thorough the fog it came;
As if it had been a Christian soul,
We hailed it in God's name.

Till a great sea-bird, called the Albatross, came through and snow-fog, and was received with great joy and hospitality.

It ate the food it ne'er had eat,
And round and round it flew.
The ice did split with a thunder-fit;
The helmsman steered us through!

And lo! the Albatross proveth a bird of good omen, and followeth the ship as it returned northward through fog and floating ice.

And a good south wind sprung up behind;
The Albatross did follow,
And every day, for food or play,
Came to the mariners' hollo!

In mist or cloud, on mast or shroud,
It perched for vespers nine;
Whiles all the night, through fog-smoke white,
Glimmered the white moon-shine.

The ancient Mariner inhospitably killeth the pious bird of good omen.

'God save thee, ancient Mariner!
From the fiends, that plague thee thus!—
Why look'st thou so?'—With my cross-bow
I shot the Albatross.

PART II

The Sun now rose upon the right:
Out of the sea came he,
Still hid in mist, and on the left
Went down into the sea.

And the good south wind still blew behind,
But no sweet bird did follow,
Nor any day for food or play
Came to the mariners' hollo!

His shipmates cry out against the ancient Mariner, for killing the bird of good luck.

And I had done a hellish thing,
And it would work 'em woe:
For all averred, I had killed the bird
That made the breeze to blow.
Ah wretch! said they, the bird to slay,
That made the breeze to blow!

Nor dim nor red, like God's own head,
The glorious Sun uprist:
Then all averred, I had killed the bird
That brought the fog and mist.
'Twas right, said they, such birds to slay,
That bring the fog and mist.

The fair breeze blew, the white foam flew,
The furrow followed free;
We were the first that ever burst
Into that silent sea.

Down dropt the breeze, the sails dropt down,
'Twas sad as sad could be;
And we did speak only to break
The silence of the sea!

All in a hot and copper sky,
The bloody Sun, at noon,
Right up above the mast did stand,
No bigger than the Moon.

Day after day, day after day,
We stuck, nor breath nor motion;
As idle as a painted ship
Upon a painted ocean.

Water, water, every where,
And all the boards did shrink;
Water, water, every where,
Nor any drop to drink.

The very deep did rot: O Christ!
That ever this should be!
Yea, slimy things did crawl with legs
Upon the slimy sea.

But when the fog cleared off, they justify the same, and thus make themselves accomplices in the crime.

The fair breeze continues; the ship enters the Pacific Ocean, and sails northward, even till it reaches the Line.

The ship hath been suddenly becalmed.

And the Albatross begins to be avenged.

25

About, about, in reel and rout
The death-fires danced at night;
The water, like a witch's oils,
Burnt green, and blue and white.

And some in dreams assured were
Of the spirit that plagued us so;
Nine fathom deep he had followed us
From the land of mist and snow.

And every tongue, through utter drought,
Was withered at the root;
We could not speak, no more than if
We had been choked with soot.

Ah! well a-day! what evil looks
Had I from old and young!
Instead of the cross, the Albatross
About my neck was hung.

PART III

There passed a weary time. Each throat
Was parched, and glazed each eye.
A weary time! a weary time,
How glazed each weary eye,
When looking westward, I beheld
A something in the sky.

At first it seemed a little speck,
And then it seemed a mist;
It moved and moved, and took at last
A certain shape, I wist.

A speck, a mist, a shape, I wist!
And still it neared and neared:
As if it dodged a water-sprite,
It plunged and tacked and veered.

With throats unslaked, with black lips baked,
We could nor laugh nor wail;
Through utter drought all dumb we stood!
I bit my arm, I sucked the blood,
And cried, A sail! a sail!

At its nearer approach, it seemeth him to be a ship; and at a dear ransom he freeth his speech from the bonds of thirst.

With throats unslaked, with black lips baked,
Agape they heard me call:
Gramercy! they for joy did grin,
And all at once their breath drew in,
As they were drinking all.

A flash of joy;

See! see! (I cried) she tacks no more!
Hither to work us weal;
Without a breeze, without a tide,
She steadies with upright keel!

And horror follows. For can it be a ship that comes onward without wind or tide?

The western wave was all a-flame.
The day was well nigh done!
Almost upon the western wave
Rested the broad bright Sun;
When that strange shape drove suddenly
Betwixt us and the Sun.

And straight the Sun was flecked with bars,
(Heaven's Mother send us grace!)
As if through a dungeon-grate he peered
With broad and burning face.

It seemeth him but the skeleton of a ship.

27

Alas! (thought I, and my heart beat loud)
How fast she nears and nears!
Are those her sails that glance in the Sun,
Like restless gossameres?

Are those her ribs through which the Sun
Did peer, as through a grate?
And is that Woman all her crew?
Is that a Death? and are there two?
Is Death that woman's mate?

Her lips were red, her looks were free,
Her locks were yellow as gold:
Her skin was as white as leprosy,
The Night-mare Life-in-Death was she,
Who thicks man's blood with cold.

The naked hulk alongside came,
And the twain were casting dice;
'The game is done! I've won, I've won!'
Quoth she, and whistles thrice.

The Sun's rim dips; the stars rush out:
At one stride comes the dark;
With far-heard whisper, o'er the sea,
Off shot the spectre-bark.

We listened and looked sideways up!
Fear at my heart, as at a cup,
My life-blood seemed to sip!
The stars were dim, and thick the night,
The steersman's face by his lamp gleamed white;
From the sails the dew did drip—
Till clomb above the eastern bar
The horned Moon, with one bright star
Within the nether tip.

28

One after one, by the star-dogged Moon,
Too quick for groan or sigh,
Each turned his face with a ghastly pang,
And cursed me with his eye.

Four times fifty living men,
(And I heard nor sigh nor groan)
With heavy thump, a lifeless lump,
They dropped down one by one.

The souls did from their bodies fly,—
They fled to bliss or woe!
And every soul, it passed me by,
Like the whizz of my cross-bow!

PART IV

'I fear thee, ancient Mariner!
I fear thy skinny hand!
And thou art long, and lank, and brown,
As is the ribbed sea-sand.[1]

I fear thee and thy glittering eye,
And thy skinny hand, so brown.'—
Fear not, fear not, thou wedding-guest!
This body dropt not down.

Alone, alone, all, all alone,
Alone on a wide wide sea!
And never a saint took pity on
My soul in agony.

[1] For the last two lines of this stanza, I am indebted to Mr. Wordsworth. It was on a delightful walk from Nether Stowey to Dulverton, with him and his sister, in the autumn of 1797, that this poem was planned, and in part composed.

He despiseth the creatures of the calm.

The many men, so beautiful!
And they all dead did lie:
And a thousand thousand slimy things
Lived on; and so did I.

And envieth that they should live, and so many lie dead.

I looked upon the rotting sea,
And drew my eyes away;
I looked upon the rotting deck,
And there the dead men lay.

I looked to heaven, and tried to pray;
But or ever a prayer had gusht,
A wicked whisper came, and made
My heart as dry as dust.

I closed my lids, and kept them close,
And the balls like pulses beat;
For the sky and the sea, and the sea and the sky
Lay like a load on my weary eye,
And the dead were at my feet.

But the curse liveth for him in the eye of the dead men.

The cold sweat melted from their limbs,
Nor rot nor reek did they:
The look with which they looked on me
Had never passed away.

An orphan's curse would drag to hell
A spirit from on high;
But oh! more horrible than that
Is the curse in a dead man's eye!
Seven days, seven nights, I saw that curse,
And yet I could not die.

30

The moving Moon went up the sky,
And no where did abide:
Softly she was going up,
And a star or two beside—

the stars that still sojourn, yet still move onward; and every where the blue sky be-
longs to them, and is their appointed rest, and their native country and their own
natural homes, which they enter unannounced, as lords that are certainly expected
and yet there is a silent joy at their arrival.

Her beams bemocked the sultry main,
Like April hoar-frost spread;
But where the ship's huge shadow lay,
The charmed water burnt alway
A still and awful red.

Beyond the shadow of the ship,
I watched the water-snakes:
They moved in tracks of shining white,
And when they reared, the elfish light
Fell off in hoary flakes.

Within the shadow of the ship
I watched their rich attire:
Blue, glossy green, and velvet black,
They coiled and swam; and every track
Was a flash of golden fire.

O happy living things! no tongue
Their beauty might declare:
A spring of love gushed from my heart,
And I blessed them unaware:
Sure my kind saint took pity on me,
And I blessed them unaware.

The selfsame moment I could pray;
And from my neck so free
The Albatross fell off, and sank
Like lead into the sea.

31

PART V

Oh sleep! it is a gentle thing,
Beloved from pole to pole!
To Mary Queen the praise be given!
She sent the gentle sleep from Heaven,
That slid into my soul.

By grace of
the holy
Mother, the
ancient Ma-
riner is re-
freshed with
rain.

The silly buckets on the deck,
That had so long remained,
I dreamt that they were filled with dew,
And when I awoke, it rained.

My lips were wet, my throat was cold,
My garments all were dank;
Sure I had drunken in my dreams,
And still my body drank.

I moved, and could not feel my limbs:
I was so light—almost
I thought that I had died in sleep,
And was a blessed ghost.

He heareth
sounds and
seeth strange
sights and
commotions
in the sky
and the ele-
ment.

And soon I heard a roaring wind:
It did not come anear;
But with its sound it shook the sails,
That were so thin and sere.

The upper air burst into life!
And a hundred fire-flags sheen,
To and fro they were hurried about!
And to and fro, and in and out,
The wan stars danced between.

And the coming wind did roar more loud,
And the sails did sigh like sedge;
And the rain poured down from one black cloud·
The Moon was at its edge.

The thick black cloud was cleft, and still
The Moon was at its side:
Like waters shot from some high crag,
The lightning fell with never a jag,
A river steep and wide.

The loud wind never reached the ship,
Yet now the ship moved on!
Beneath the lightning and the moon
The dead men gave a groan.

The bodies of
the ship's
crew are
inspired, and
the ship
moves on.

They groaned, they stirred, they all uprose,
Nor spake, nor moved their eyes;
It had been strange, even in a dream,
To have seen those dead men rise.

The helmsman steered, the ship moved on;
Yet never a breeze up blew;
The mariners all 'gan work the ropes,
Where they were wont to do;
They raised their limbs like lifeless tools—
We were a ghastly crew.

The body of my brother's son
Stood by me, knee to knee:
The body and I pulled at one rope,
But he said nought to me.

'I fear thee, ancient Mariner!'
Be calm, thou Wedding-Guest!
'Twas not those souls that fled in pain,
Which to their corses came again,
But a troop of spirits blest:

For when it dawned—they dropped their arms,
And clustered round the mast;
Sweet sounds rose slowly through their mouths
And from their bodies passed.

Around, around, flew each sweet sound,
Then darted to the Sun;
Slowly the sounds came back again,
Now mixed, now one by one.

Sometimes a-dropping from the sky
I heard the sky-lark sing;
Sometimes all little birds that are,
How they seemed to fill the sea and air
With their sweet jargoning!

And now 'twas like all instruments,
Now like a lonely flute;
And now it is an angel's song,
That makes the heavens be mute.

It ceased; yet still the sails made on
A pleasant noise till noon,
A noise like of a hidden brook
In the leafy month of June,
That to the sleeping woods all night
Singeth a quiet tune.

Till noon we quietly sailed on,
Yet never a breeze did breathe:
Slowly and smoothly went the ship,
Moved onward from beneath.

Under the keel nine fathom deep,
From the land of mist and snow,
The spirit slid: and it was he
That made the ship to go.
The sails at noon left off their tune,
And the ship stood still also.

The lonesome
spirit from
the south
pole carries
on the ship
as far as the
Line, in obe-
dience to the
angelic
troop, but
still requireth
vengeance.

The Sun, right up above the mast,
Had fixed her to the ocean:
But in a minute she 'gan stir,
With a short uneasy motion—
Backwards and forwards half her length
With a short uneasy motion.

Then like a pawing horse let go,
She made a sudden bound:
It flung the blood into my head,
And I fell down in a swound.

How long in that same fit I lay,
I have not to declare;
But ere my living life returned,
I heard, and in my soul discerned
Two voices in the air.

The Polar
Spirit's fel-
low demons,
the invisible
inhabitants
of the ele-
ment, take
part in his
wrong; and
two of them
relate, one to
the other,
that penance
long and hea-
vy for the an-
cient Mari-
ner hath been
accorded to
the Polar
Spirit, who
returneth
southward.

'Is it he?' quoth one, 'Is this the man?
By him who died on cross,
With his cruel bow he laid full low
The harmless Albatross.

The spirit who bideth by himself
In the land of mist and snow,
He loved the bird that loved the man
Who shot him with his bow.'

The other was a softer voice,
As soft as honey-dew:
Quoth he, 'The man hath penance done,
And penance more will do.'

PART VI

FIRST VOICE

But tell me, tell me! speak again,
Thy soft response renewing—
What makes that ship drive on so fast?
What is the ocean doing?

SECOND VOICE

Still as a slave before his lord,
The ocean hath no blast;
His great bright eye most silently
Up to the Moon is cast—

If he may know which way to go;
For she guides him smooth or grim.
See, brother, see! how graciously
She looketh down on him.

FIRST VOICE

The Mariner
hath been
cast into a

But why drives on that ship so fast,
Without or wave or wind?

36

The air is cut away before,
And closes from behind.

Fly, brother, fly! more high, more high!
Or we shall be belated:
For slow and slow that ship will go,
When the Mariner's trance is abated.

I woke, and we were sailing on
As in a gentle weather:
'Twas night, calm night, the moon was high;
The dead men stood together.

All stood together on the deck,
For a charnel-dungeon fitter:
All fixed on me their stony eyes,
That in the Moon did glitter.

The pang, the curse, with which they died,
Had never passed away:
I could not draw my eyes from theirs,
Nor turn them up to pray.

And now this spell was snapt: once more
I viewed the ocean green,
And looked far forth, yet little saw
Of what had else been seen—

Like one, that on a lonesome road
Doth walk in fear and dread,
And having once turned round walks on,
And turns no more his head;
Because he knows, a frightful fiend
Doth close behind him tread.

trance; for the angelic power causeth the vessel to drive northward faster than human life could endure.

The supernatural motion is retarded; the Mariner awakes, and his penance begins anew.

The curse is finally expiated.

But soon there breathed a wind on me,
Nor sound nor motion made:
Its path was not upon the sea,
In ripple or in shade.

It raised my hair, it fanned my cheek
Like a meadow-gale of spring—
It mingled strangely with my fears,
Yet it felt like a welcoming.

Swiftly, swiftly flew the ship,
Yet she sailed softly too:
Sweetly, sweetly blew the breeze—
On me alone it blew.

Oh! dream of joy! is this indeed
The light-house top I see?
Is this the hill? is this the kirk?
Is this mine own countree?

We drifted o'er the harbour-bar,
And I with sobs did pray—
O let me be awake, my God!
Or let me sleep alway.

The harbour-bay was clear as glass,
So smoothly it was strewn!
And on the bay the moonlight lay,
And the shadow of the moon.

The rock shone bright, the kirk no less,
That stands above the rock:
The moonlight steeped in silentness
The steady weathercock.

And the bay was white with silent light,
Till rising from the same,
Full many shapes, that shadows were,
In crimson colours came.

The angelic
spirits leave
the dead
bodies.

A little distance from the prow
Those crimson shadows were:
I turned my eyes upon the deck—
Oh, Christ! what saw I there!

And appear
in their own
forms of light.

Each corse lay flat, lifeless and flat,
And, by the holy rood!
A man all light, a seraph-man,
On every corse there stood.

This seraph-band, each waved his hand:
It was a heavenly sight!
They stood as signals to the land,
Each one a lovely light;

This seraph-band, each waved his hand,
No voice did they impart—
No voice; but oh! the silence sank
Like music on my heart.

But soon I heard the dash of oars,
I heard the Pilot's cheer;
My head was turned perforce away,
And I saw a boat appear.

The Pilot and the Pilot's boy,
I heard them coming fast:
Dear Lord in Heaven! it was a joy
The dead men could not blast.

I saw a third—I heard his voice:
It is the Hermit good!
He singeth loud his godly hymns
That he makes in the wood.
He'll shrieve my soul, he'll wash away
The Albatross's blood.

PART VII

The Hermit
of the wood.

This Hermit good lives in that wood
Which slopes down to the sea.
How loudly his sweet voice he rears!
He loves to talk with marineres
That come from a far countree.

He kneels at morn, and noon, and eve—
He hath a cushion plump:
It is the moss that wholly hides
The rotted old oak-stump.

The skiff-boat neared: I heard them talk,
'Why, this is strange, I trow!
Where are those lights so many and fair,
That signal made but now?'

Approacheth
the ship with
wonder.

'Strange, by my faith!' the Hermit said—
'And they answered not our cheer!
The planks looked warped! and see those sails,
How thin they are and sere!
I never saw aught like to them,
Unless perchance it were

Brown skeletons of leaves that lag
My forest-brook along;
When the ivy-tod is heavy with snow,
And the owlet whoops to the wolf below,
That eats the she-wolf's young.'

'Dear Lord! it hath a fiendish look—
(The Pilot made reply)
I am a-feared'—'Push on, push on!'
Said the Hermit cheerily.

The boat came closer to the ship,
But I nor spake nor stirred;
The boat came close beneath the ship,
And straight a sound was heard.

Under the water it rumbled on,
Still louder and more dread:
It reached the ship, it split the bay;
The ship went down like lead.

The ship suddenly sinketh.

Stunned by that loud and dreadful sound,
Which sky and ocean smote,
Like one that hath been seven days drowned
My body lay afloat;
But swift as dreams, myself I found
Within the Pilot's boat.

The ancient Mariner is saved in the Pilot's boat.

Upon the whirl, where sank the ship,
The boat spun round and round;
And all was still, save that the hill
Was telling of the sound.

I moved my lips—the Pilot shrieked
And fell down in a fit;
The holy Hermit raised his eyes,
And prayed where he did sit.

I took the oars: the Pilot's boy,
Who now doth crazy go,
Laughed loud and long, and all the while
His eyes went to and fro.
'Ha! ha!' quoth he, 'full plain I see,
The Devil knows how to row.'

And now, all in my own countree,
I stood on the firm land!
The Hermit stepped forth from the boat,
And scarcely he could stand.

The ancient Mariner earnestly entreateth the Hermit to shrieve him; and the penance of life falls on him.

'O shrieve me, shrieve me, holy man!'
The Hermit crossed his brow.
'Say quick,' quoth he, 'I bid thee say—
What manner of man art thou?'

Forthwith this frame of mine was wrenched
With a woful agony,
Which forced me to begin my tale;
And then it left me free.

And ever and anon throughout his future life an agony constraineth him to travel from land to land.

Since then, at an uncertain hour,
That agony returns:
And till my ghastly tale is told,
This heart within me burns.

42

I pass, like night, from land to land;
I have strange power of speech;
That moment that his face I see,
I know the man that must hear me:
To him my tale I teach.

What loud uproar bursts from that door
The wedding-guests are there:
But in the garden-bower the bride
And bride-maids singing are:
And hark the little vesper bell,
Which biddeth me to prayer!

O Wedding-Guest! this soul hath been
Alone on a wide wide sea:
So lonely 'twas, that God himself
Scarce seemed there to be.

O sweeter than the marriage-feast,
'Tis sweeter far to me,
To walk together to the kirk
With a goodly company!—

To walk together to the kirk,
And all together pray,
While each to his great Father bends,
Old men, and babes, and loving friends,
And youths and maidens gay!

Farewell, farewell! but this I tell
To thee, thou Wedding-Guest!
He prayeth well, who loveth well
Both man and bird and beast.

And to teach,
by his own
example,
love and re-
verence to all
things that
God made
and loveth.

43

He prayeth best, who loveth best
All things both great and small;
For the dear God who loveth us,
He made and loveth all.

The Mariner, whose eye is bright,
Whose beard with age is hoar,
Is gone: and now the Wedding-Guest
Turned from the bridegroom's door.

He went like one that hath been stunned,
And is of sense forlorn:
A sadder and a wiser man,
He rose the morrow morn.

On a Ruined House in a Romantic Country

And this reft house is that the which he built,
Lamented Jack! And here his malt he pil'd,
Cautious in vain! These rats that squeak so wild,
Squeak, not unconscious of their father's guilt.
Did ye not see her gleaming thro' the glade?
Belike, 'twas she, the maiden all forlorn.
What though she milk no cow with crumpled horn,
Yet *aye* she haunts the dale where *erst* she stray'd;
And *aye* beside her stalks her amorous knight!
Still on his thighs their wonted brogues are worn,   10
And thro' those brogues, still tatter'd and betorn,
His hindward charms gleam an unearthly white;
As when thro' broken clouds at night's high noon
Peeps in fair fragments forth the full-orb'd harvest-moon!

Christabel

PREFACE

THE first part of the following poem was written in the year 1797, at Stowey, in the county of Somerset. The second part, after my return from Germany, in the year 1800, at Keswick, Cumberland. It is probable, that if the poem had been finished at either of the former periods, or if even the first and second part had been published in the year 1800, the impression of its originality would have been much greater than I dare at present expect. But for this, I have only my own indolence to blame. The dates are mentioned for the exclusive purpose of precluding charges of plagiarism or servile imitation from myself. For there is amongst us a set of critics, who seem to hold, that every possible thought and image is traditional; who have no notion that there are such things as fountains in the world, small as well as great; and who would therefore charitably derive every rill they behold flowing, from a perforation made in some other man's tank. I am confident, however, that as far as the present poem is concerned, the celebrated poets whose writings I might be suspected of having imitated, either in particular passages, or in the tone and the spirit of the whole, would be among the first to vindicate me from the charge, and who, on any striking coincidence, would permit me to address them in this doggerel version of two monkish Latin hexameters.

> 'Tis mine and it is likewise yours;
> But an if this will not do;
> Let it be mine, good friend! for I
> Am the poorer of the two.

I have only to add, that the metre of the Christabel is not, properly speaking, irregular, though it may seem so from its being founded on a new principle: namely, that of counting in each line the accents, not the syllables. Though the latter may vary from seven to twelve, yet in each line the accents will be found to be only four. Nevertheless this occasional variation in number of syllables is not introduced wantonly, or for the mere ends of convenience, but in correspondence with some transition, in the nature of the imagery or passion.

PART I

'Tis the middle of night by the castle clock,
And the owls have awakened the crowing cock;
Tu—whit!——Tu—whoo!
And hark, again! the crowing cock,
How drowsily it crew.   5

Sir Leoline, the Baron rich,
Hath a toothless mastiff bitch;
From her kennel beneath the rock
She maketh answer to the clock,
Four for the quarters, and twelve for the hour;   10
Ever and aye, by shine and shower,
Sixteen short howls, not over loud;
Some say, she sees my lady's shroud.

Is the night chilly and dark?
The night is chilly, but not dark.   15
The thin gray cloud is spread on high,
It covers but not hides the sky.
The moon is behind, and at the full;
And yet she looks both small and dull.
The night is chill, the cloud is gray: 20
'Tis a month before the month of May
And the Spring comes slowly up this way

The lovely lady, Christabel,
Whom her father loves so well,
What makes her in the wood so late,   25
A furlong from the castle gate?

She had dreams all yesternight
Of her own betrothed knight;
And she in the midnight wood will pray
For the weal of her lover that's far away.   30

She stole along, she nothing spoke,
The sighs she heaved were soft and low,
And naught was green upon the oak,
But moss and rarest mistletoe:
She kneels beneath the huge oak tree,   35
And in silence prayeth she.

The lady sprang up suddenly,
The lovely lady, Christabel!
It moaned as near, as near can be,
But what it is, she cannot tell.—   40
On the other side it seems to be,
Of the huge, broad-breasted, old oak tree.

The night is chill; the forest bare;
Is it the wind that moaneth bleak?
There is not wind enough in the air   45
To move away the ringlet curl
From the lovely lady's cheek—
There is not wind enough to twirl
The one red leaf, the last of its clan,
That dances as often as dance it can,   50
Hanging so light, and hanging so high,
On the topmost twig that looks up at the sky

Hush, beating heart of Christabel!
Jesu, Maria, shield her well!
She folded her arms beneath her cloak,   55
And stole to the other side of the oak.
    What sees she there?

There she sees a damsel bright,
Drest in a silken robe of white,
That shadowy in the moonlight shone: 60
The neck that made that white robe wan,
Her stately neck, and arms were bare;
Her blue-veined feet unsandal'd were,
And wildly glittered here and there
The gems entangled in her hair.   65
I guess, 'twas frightful there to see
A lady so richly clad as she—
Beautiful exceedingly!

Mary mother, save me now!
(Said Christabel,) And who art thou?   70

The lady strange made answer meet,
And her voice was faint and sweet:—
Have pity on my sore distress,
I scarce can speak for weariness:
Stretch forth thy hand, and have no fear!   75
Said Christabel, How camest thou here?
And the lady, whose voice was faint and sweet,
Did thus pursue her answer meet:—

My sire is of a noble line,
And my name is Geraldine: 80
Five warriors seized me yestermorn,
Me, even me, a maid forlorn:
They choked my cries with force and fright,
And tied me on a palfrey white.
The palfrey was as fleet as wind,   85
And they rode furiously behind.
They spurred amain, their steeds were white:
And once we crossed the shade of night.

As sure as Heaven shall rescue me,
I have no thought what men they be;   90
Nor do I know how long it is
(For I have lain entranced I wis)
Since one, the tallest of the five,
Took me from the palfrey's back,
A weary woman, scarce alive.   95
Some muttered words his comrades spoke:
He placed me underneath this oak;
He swore they would return with haste;
Whither they went I cannot tell—
I thought I heard, some minutes past,   100
Sounds as of a castle bell.
Stretch forth thy hand (thus ended she),
And help a wretched maid to flee.

Then Christabel stretched forth her hand
And comforted fair Geraldine: 105
O well, bright dame! may you command
The service of Sir Leoline;
And gladly our stout chivalry
Will he send forth and friends withal
To guide and guard you safe and free   110
Home to your noble father's hall.

She rose: and forth with steps they passed
That strove to be, and were not, fast.
Her gracious stars the lady blest,
And this spake on sweet Christabel: 115
All our household are at rest,
The hall as silent as the cell;
Sir Leoline is weak in health,
And may not well awakened be,
But we will move as if in stealth,   120

And I beseech your courtesy,
This night, to share your couch with me.

They crossed the moat, and Christabel
Took the key that fitted well;
A little door she opened straight,   125
All in the middle of the gate;
The gate that was ironed within and without,
Where an army in battle array had marched out.
The lady sank, belike through pain,
And Christabel with might and main   130
Lifted her up, a weary weight,
Over the threshold of the gate:
Then the lady rose again,
And moved, as she were not in pain.

So free from danger, free from fear,   135
They crossed the court: right glad they were.
And Christabel devoutly cried
To the Lady by her side;
Praise we the Virgin all divine
Who hath rescued thee from thy distress!   140
Alas, alas! said Geraldine,
I cannot speak for weariness.
So free from danger, free from fear,
They crossed the court: right glad they were.

Outside her kennel the mastiff old   145
Lay fast asleep, in moonshine cold.
The mastiff old did not awake,
Yet she an angry moan did make!
And what can ail the mastiff bitch?
Never till now she uttered yell   150
Beneath the eye of Christabel.

Perhaps it is the owlet's scritch:
For what can ail the mastiff bitch?

They passed the hall, that echoes still,
Pass as lightly as you will!   155
The brands were flat, the brands were dying,
Amid their own white ashes lying;
But when the lady passed, there came
A tongue of light, a fit of flame;
And Christabel saw the lady's eye,   160
And nothing else saw she thereby,
Save the boss of the shield of Sir Leoline tall,
Which hung in a murky old niche in the wall.
O softly tread, said Christabel,
My father seldom sleepeth well.   165

Sweet Christabel her feet doth bare,
And, jealous of the listening air,
They steal their way from stair to stair,
Now in glimmer, and now in gloom,
And now they pass the Baron's room,   170
As still as death with stifled breath!
And now have reached her chamber door;
And now doth Geraldine press down
The rushes of the chamber floor.

The moon shines dim in the open air,   175
And not a moonbeam enters here.
But they without its light can see
The chamber carved so curiously,
Carved with figures strange and sweet,
All made out of the carver's brain,   180
For a lady's chamber meet:
The lamp with twofold silver chain
Is fastened to an angel's feet.

The silver lamp burns dead and dim;
But Christabel the lamp will trim.   185
She trimmed the lamp, and made it bright,
And left it swinging to and fro,
While Geraldine, in wretched plight,
Sank down upon the floor below.

O weary lady, Geraldine,   190
I pray you, drink this cordial wine!
It is a wine of virtuous powers;
My mother made it of wild flowers.

And will your mother pity me,
Who am a maiden most forlorn?   195
Christabel answered—Woe is me!
She died the hour that I was born.
I have heard the grey-haired friar tell,
How on her death-bed she did say,
That she should hear the castle-bell   200
Strike twelve upon my wedding day.
O mother dear! that thou wert here!
I would, said Geraldine, she were!
But soon with altered voice, she said—
'Off, wandering mother! Peak and pine!   205
I have power to bid thee flee.'
Alas! what ails poor Geraldine?

Why stares she with unsettled eye?
Can she the bodiless dead espy?
And why with hollow voice cries she,   210
'Off, woman, off! this hour is mine—
Though thou her guardian spirit be,
Off, woman, off! 'tis given to me.'

Then Christabel knelt by the lady's side,
And raised to heaven her eyes so blue—   215
Alas! said she, this ghastly ride—
Dear lady! it hath wildered you!
The lady wiped her moist cold brow,
And faintly said, ' 'tis over now!'

Again the wild-flower wine she drank: 220
Her fair large eyes 'gan glitter bright,
And from the floor whereon she sank,
The lofty lady stood upright;
She was most beautiful to see,
Like a lady of a far countrée.   225

And thus the lofty lady spake—
All they, who live in the upper sky,
Do love you, holy Christabel!
And you love them, and for their sake
And for the good which me befell,   230
Even I in my degree will try,
Fair maiden, to requite you well.
But now unrobe yourself; for I
Must pray, ere yet in bed I lie.

Quoth Christabel, so let it be!   235
And as the lady bade, did she.
Her gentle limbs did she undress,
And lay down in her loveliness.

But through her brain of weal and woe
So many thoughts moved to and fro,   240

That vain it were her lids to close;
So half-way from the bed she rose,
And on her elbow did recline
To look at the lady Geraldine.

Beneath the lamp the lady bowed,   245
And slowly rolled her eyes around;
Then drawing in her breath aloud
Like one that shuddered, she unbound
The cincture from beneath her breast:
Her silken robe, and inner vest,   250
Dropt to her feet, and full in view,
Behold! her bosom and half her side——
A sight to dream of, not to tell!
O shield her! shield sweet Christabel!

Yet Geraldine nor speaks nor stirs;   255
Ah! what a stricken look was hers!
Deep from within she seems half-way
To lift some weight with sick assay,
And eyes the maid and seeks delay;
Then suddenly as one defied   260
Collects herself in scorn and pride,
And lay down by the maiden's side!—
And in her arms the maid she took,
          Ah well-a-day!
And with low voice and doleful look   265
These words did say:
In the touch of this bosom there worketh a spell,
Which is lord of thy utterance, Christabel!
Thou knowest to-night, and wilt know to-morrow
This mark of my shame, this seal of my sorrow;   270

But vainly thou warrest,
　　For this is alone in
Thy power to declare,
　　That in the dim forest
　　Thou heard'st a low moaning,　　　　　275
And found'st a bright lady, surpassingly fair:
And didst bring her home with thee in love and in charity,
To shield her and shelter her from the damp air.

THE CONCLUSION TO PART I

It was a lovely sight to see
The lady Christabel, when she　　　　　　280
Was praying at the old oak tree.
　　Amid the jagged shadows
　　Of mossy leafless boughs,
　　Kneeling in the moonlight,
　　To make her gentle vows;　　　　　　285
Her slender palms together prest,
Heaving sometimes on her breast;
Her face resigned to bliss or bale—
Her face, oh call it fair not pale,
And both blue eyes more bright than clear,　　290
Each about to have a tear.

With open eyes (ah woe is me!)
Asleep, and dreaming fearfully,
Fearfully dreaming, yet I wis,
Dreaming that alone, which is—　　　　　295
O sorrow and shame! Can this be she,
The lady, who knelt at the old oak tree?
And lo! the worker of these harms,
That holds the maiden in her arms,

Seems to slumber still and mild,   300
As a mother with her child.

A star hath set, a star hath risen,
O Geraldine! since arms of thine
Have been the lovely lady's prison.
O Geraldine! one hour was thine—   305
Thou'st had thy will! By tairn and rill,
The night-birds all that hour were still.
But now they are jubilant anew,
From cliff and tower, tu—whoo! tu—whoo!
Tu—whoo! tu—whoo! from wood and fell!   310
And see! the lady Christabel

Gathers herself from out her trance;
Her limbs relax, her countenance
Grows sad and soft; the smooth thin lids
Close o'er her eyes; and tears she sheds—   315
Large tears that leave the lashes bright!
And oft the while she seems to smile
As infants at a sudden light!
Yea, she doth smile, and she doth weep,
Like a youthful hermitess,   320
Beauteous in a wilderness,
Who, praying always, prays in sleep.
And, if she move unquietly,
Perchance, 'tis but the blood so free,
Comes back and tingles in her feet.   325
No doubt, she hath a vision sweet.
What if her guardian spirit 'twere?
What if she knew her mother near?
But this she knows, in joys and woes,
That saints will aid if men will call: 330
For the blue sky bends over all!

PART II

Each matin bell, the Baron saith,
Knells us back to a world of death.
These words Sir Leoline first said,
When he rose and found his lady dead: 335
These words Sir Leoline will say,
Many a morn to his dying day!

And hence the custom and law began,
That still at dawn the sacristan,
Who duly pulls the heavy bell,   340
Five and forty beads must tell
Between each stroke—a warning knell,
Which not a soul can choose but hear
From Bratha Head to Wyndermere.
Saith Bracy the bard, So let it knell!   345
And let the drowsy sacristan
Still count as slowly as he can!
There is no lack of such, I ween,
As well fill up the space between.
In Langdale Pike and Witch's Lair,   350
And Dungeon-ghyll so foully rent,
With ropes of rock and bells of air
Three sinful sextons' ghosts are pent,
Who all give back, one after t'other,
The death-note to their living brother;   355
And oft too, by the knell offended,
Just as their one! two! three! is ended,
The devil mocks the doleful tale
With a merry peal from Borodale.

The air is still! through mist and cloud 360
That merry peal comes ringing loud;
And Geraldine shakes off her dread,
And rises lightly from the bed;
Puts on her silken vestments white,
And tricks her hair in lovely plight, 365
And nothing doubting of her spell
Awakens the lady Christabel.
'Sleep you, sweet lady Christabel?
I trust that you have rested well.'

And Christabel awoke and spied 370
The same who lay down by her side—
O rather say, the same whom she
Raised up beneath the old oak tree!
Nay, fairer yet! and yet more fair!
For she belike hath drunken deep 375
Of all the blessedness of sleep!
And while she spake, her looks, her air
Such gentle thankfulness declare,
That (so it seemed) her girded vests
Grew tight beneath her heaving breasts. 380

'Sure I have sinned!' said Christabel,
'Now heaven be praised if all be well!'
And in low faltering tones, yet sweet,
Did she the lofty lady greet
With such perplexity of mind 385
As dreams too lively leave behind.

So quickly she rose, and quickly arrayed
Her maiden limbs, and having prayed
That He, who on the cross did groan,
Might wash away her sins unknown, 390

She forthwith led fair Geraldine
To meet her sire, Sir Leoline.

The lovely maid and the lady tall
Are pacing both into the hall,
And pacing on through page and groom,   395
Enter the Baron's presence room.
The Baron rose, and while he prest
His gentle daughter to his breast,
With cheerful wonder in his eyes
The lady Geraldine espies,   400
And gave such welcome to the same,
As might beseem so bright a dame!

But when he heard the lady's tale,
And when she told her father's name,
Why waxed Sir Leoline so pale,   405
Murmuring o'er the name again,
Lord Roland de Vaux of Tryermaine?

Alas! they had been friends in youth;
But whispering tongues can poison truth;
And constancy lives in realms above;   410
And life is thorny; and youth is vain;
And to be wroth with one we love,
Doth work like madness in the brain.
And thus it chanced, as I divine,
With Roland and Sir Leoline.   415

Each spake words of high disdain
And insult to his heart's best brother:
They parted—ne'er to meet again!
But never either found another

To free the hollow heart from paining— 420
They stood aloof, the scars remaining,
Like cliffs which had been rent asunder;
A dreary sea now flows between;—
But neither heat, nor frost, nor thunder,
Shall wholly do away, I ween, 425
The marks of that which once hath been.

Sir Leoline, a moment's space,
Stood gazing on the damsel's face:
And the youthful Lord of Tryermaine
Came back upon his heart again. 430

O then the Baron forgot his age,
His noble heart swelled high with rage;
He swore by the wounds in Jesu's side,
He would proclaim it far and wide
With trump and solemn heraldry, 435
That they who thus had wronged the dame,
Were base as spotted infamy!
'And if they dare deny the same,
My herald shall appoint a week,
And let the recreant traitors seek 440
My tourney court—that there and then
I may dislodge their reptile souls
From the bodies and forms of men!'
He spake: his eye in lightning rolls!
For the lady was ruthlessly seized; and he kenned 445
In the beautiful lady the child of his friend!

And now the tears were on his face,
And fondly in his arms he took
Fair Geraldine, who met the embrace,
Prolonging it with joyous look. 450

Which when she viewed, a vision fell
Upon the soul of Christabel,
The vision of fear, the touch and pain!
She shrunk and shuddered, and saw again—
(Ah, woe is me! Was it for thee,   455
Thou gentle maid! such sights to see?)
Again she saw that bosom old,
Again she felt that bosom cold,
And drew in her breath with a hissing sound:
Whereat the Knight turned wildly round,   460
And nothing saw, but his own sweet maid
With eyes upraised, as one that prayed.

The touch, the sight, had passed away,
And in its stead that vision blest,
Which comforted her after-rest,   465
While in the lady's arms she lay,
Had put a rapture in her breast,
And on her lips and o'er her eyes
Spread smiles like light!
                              With new surprise,
'What ails then my beloved child?'   470
The Baron said—His daughter mild
Made answer, 'All will yet be well!'
I ween, she had no power to tell
Aught else: so mighty was the spell.

Yet he, who saw this Geraldine,   475
Had deemed her sure a thing divine.
Such sorrow with such grace she blended,
As if she feared, she had offended
Sweet Christabel, that gentle maid!
And with such lowly tones she prayed,   480

She might be sent without delay
Home to her father's mansion.
                                        'Nay!
Nay, by my soul!' said Leoline.
'Ho! Bracy, the bard, the charge be thine!
Go thou, with music sweet and loud,   485
And take two steeds with trappings proud,
And take the youth whom thou lov'st best
To bear thy harp, and learn thy song,
And clothe you both in solemn vest,
And over the mountains haste along,   490
Lest wandering folk, that are abroad,
Detain you on the valley road.
And when he has crossed the Irthing flood,
My merry bard! he hastes, he hastes
Up Knorren Moor, through Halegarth Wood,   495
And reaches soon that castle good
Which stands and threatens Scotland's wastes.

'Bard Bracy! bard Bracy! your horses are fleet,
Ye must ride up the hall, your music so sweet,
More loud than your horses' echoing feet!   500
And loud and loud to Lord Roland call,
Thy daughter is safe in Langdale hall!
Thy beautiful daughter is safe and free—
Sir Leoline greets thee thus through me.
He bids thee come without delay   505
With all thy numerous array;
And take thy lovely daughter home:
And he will meet thee on the way
With all his numerous array
White with their panting palfreys' foam: 510
And by mine honour! I will say,
That I repent me of the day

When I spake words of fierce disdain
To Roland de Vaux of Tryermaine!—
—For since that evil hour hath flown, 515
Many a summer's sun hath shone;
Yet ne'er found I a friend again
Like Roland de Vaux of Tryermaine.'

The lady fell, and clasped his knees,
Her face upraised, her eyes o'erflowing; 520
And Bracy replied, with faltering voice,
His gracious hail on all bestowing!—
'Thy words, thou sire of Christabel,
Are sweeter than my harp can tell;
Yet might I gain a boon of thee, 525
This day my journey should not be,
So strange a dream hath come to me;
That I had vowed with music loud
To clear yon wood from thing unblest,
Warned by a vision in my rest! 530
For in my sleep I saw that dove,
That gentle bird, whom thou dost love,
And call'st by thy own daughter's name—
Sir Leoline! I saw the same
Fluttering, and uttering fearful moan, 535
Among the green herbs in the forest alone.
Which when I saw and when I heard,
I wonder'd what might ail the bird;
For nothing near it could I see,
Save the grass and green herbs underneath the old tree. 540

'And in my dream methought I went
To search out what might there be found;
And what the sweet bird's trouble meant,
That thus lay fluttering on the ground.

I went and peered, and could descry 545
No cause for her distressful cry;
But yet for her dear lady's sake
I stooped, methought, the dove to take,
When lo! I saw a bright green snake
Coiled around its wings and neck, 550
Green as the herbs on which it couched,
Close by the dove's its head it crouched;
And with the dove it heaves and stirs,
Swelling its neck as she swelled hers!
I woke; it was the midnight hour, 555
The clock was echoing in the tower;
But though my slumber was gone by,
This dream it would not pass away—
It seems to live upon my eye!
And thence I vowed this self-same day, 560
With music strong and saintly song
To wander through the forest bare,
Lest aught unholy loiter there.'

Thus Bracy said: the Baron, the while,
Half-listening heard him with a smile; 565
Then turned to Lady Geraldine,
His eyes made up of wonder and love;
And said in courtly accents fine,
'Sweet maid, Lord Roland's beauteous dove,
With arms more strong than harp or song, 570
Thy sire and I will crush the snake!'
He kissed her forehead as he spake,
And Geraldine, in maiden wise,
Casting down her large bright eyes,
With blushing cheek and courtesy fine 575
She turned her from Sir Leoline;

Softly gathering up her train,
That o'er her right arm fell again;
And folded her arms across her chest,
And couched her head upon her breast,   580
And looked askance at Christabel——
Jesu, Maria, shield her well!

A snake's small eye blinks dull and shy,
And the lady's eyes they shrunk in her head,
Each shrunk up to a serpent's eye,   585
And with somewhat of malice, and more of dread,
At Christabel she looked askance!—
One moment—and the sight was fled!
But Christabel in dizzy trance
Stumbling on the unsteady ground   590
Shuddered aloud, with a hissing sound;
And Geraldine again turned round,
And like a thing, that sought relief,
Full of wonder and full of grief,
She rolled her large bright eyes divine   595
Wildly on Sir Leoline.

The maid, alas! her thoughts are gone,
She nothing sees—no sight but one!
The maid, devoid of guile and sin,
I know not how, in fearful wise   600
So deeply had she drunken in
That look, those shrunken serpent eyes,
That all her features were resigned
To this sole image in her mind;
And passively did imitate   605
That look of dull and treacherous hate
And thus she stood, in dizzy trance,
Still picturing that look askance

With forced unconscious sympathy
Full before her father's view——   610
As far as such a look could be,
In eyes so innocent and blue!
And when the trance was o'er, the maid
Paused awhile, and inly prayed:
Then falling at the Baron's feet,   615
'By my mother's soul do I entreat
That thou this woman send away!'
She said: and more she could not say:
For what she knew she could not tell,
O'er-mastered by the mighty spell.   620

Why is thy cheek so wan and wild,
Sir Leoline? Thy only child
Lies at thy feet, thy joy, thy pride,
So fair, so innocent, so mild;
The same, for whom thy lady died!   625
O by the pangs of her dear mother
Think thou no evil of thy child!
For her, and thee, and for no other,
She prayed the moment ere she died:
Prayed that the babe for whom she died,   630
Might prove her dear lord's joy and pride!
    That prayer her deadly pangs beguiled,
            Sir Leoline!
    And wouldst thou wrong thy only child,
            Her child and thine?   635

Within the Baron's heart and brain
If thoughts, like these, had any share,
They only swelled his rage and pain,
And did but work confusion there.

His heart was cleft with pain and rage,   640
His cheeks they quivered, his eyes were wild,
Dishonoured thus in his old age;
Dishonoured by his only child,
And all his hospitality
To the wrong'd daughter of his friend   645
By more than woman's jealousy
Brought thus to a disgraceful end—
He rolled his eye with stern regard
Upon the gentle minstrel bard,
And said in tones abrupt, austere—   650
'Why, Bracy! dost thou loiter here?
I bade thee hence!' The bard obeyed;
And turning from his own sweet maid,
The aged knight, Sir Leoline,
Led forth the lady Geraldine!   655

THE CONCLUSION TO PART II

A little child, a limber elf,
Singing, dancing to itself,
A fairy thing with red round cheeks,
That always finds, and never seeks,
Makes such a vision to the sight   660
As fills a father's eyes with light;
And pleasures flow in so thick and fast
Upon his heart, that he at last
Must needs express his love's excess
With words of unmeant bitterness.   665
Perhaps 'tis pretty to force together
Thoughts so all unlike each other;
To mutter and mock a broken charm,
To dally with wrong that does no harm.

Perhaps 'tis tender too and pretty   670
At each wild word to feel within
A sweet recoil of love and pity.
And what, if in a world of sin
(O sorrow and shame should this be true!)
Such giddiness of heart and brain   675
Comes seldom save from rage and pain,
So talks as it's most used to do.

Frost at Midnight

The frost performs its secret ministry,
Unhelped by any wind. The owlet's cry
Came loud—and hark, again! loud as before.
The inmates of my cottage, all at rest,
Have left me to that solitude, which suits   5
Abstruser musings: save that at my side
My cradled infant slumbers peacefully.
'Tis calm indeed! so calm, that it disturbs
And vexes meditation with its strange
And extreme silentness. Sea, hill, and wood,   10
This populous village! Sea, and hill, and wood,
With all the numberless goings on of life,
Inaudible as dreams! the thin blue flame
Lies on my low burnt fire, and quivers not;
Only that film, which fluttered on the grate,   15
Still flutters there, the sole unquiet thing.
Methinks, its motion in this hush of nature
Gives it dim sympathies with me who live,
Making it a companionable form,
Whose puny flaps and freaks the idling Spirit   20
By its own moods interprets, every where

Echo or mirror seeking of itself,
And makes a toy of Thought.

　　　　　　　But O! how oft,
How oft, at school, with most believing mind,
Presageful, have I gazed upon the bars,　　　　　25
To watch that fluttering stranger! and as oft
With unclosed lids, already had I dreamt
Of my sweet birth-place, and the old church-tower,
Whose bells, the poor man's only music, rang
From morn to evening, all the hot Fair-day,　　　30
So sweetly, that they stirred and haunted me
With a wild pleasure, falling on mine ear
Most like articulate sounds of things to come!
So gazed I, till the soothing things I dreamt
Lulled me to sleep, and sleep prolonged my dreams!　35
And so I brooded all the following morn,
Awed by the stern preceptor's face, mine eye
Fixed with mock study on my swimming book:
Save if the door half opened, and I snatched
A hasty glance, and still my heart leaped up,　　40
For still I hoped to see the stranger's face,
Townsman, or aunt, or sister more beloved,
My play-mate when we both were clothed alike!

　Dear Babe, that sleepest cradled by my side,
Whose gentle breathings, heard in this deep calm,　45
Fill up the interspersed vacancies
And momentary pauses of the thought!
My babe so beautiful! it thrills my heart
With tender gladness, thus to look at thee,
And think that thou shalt learn far other lore　　50
And in far other scenes! For I was reared
In the great city, pent 'mid cloisters dim,
And saw nought lovely but the sky and stars.

But thou, my babe! shalt wander like a breeze
By lakes and sandy shores, beneath the crags   55
Of ancient mountain, and beneath the clouds,
Which image in their bulk both lakes and shores
And mountain crags: so shalt thou see and hear
The lovely shapes and sounds intelligible
Of that eternal language, which thy God   60
Utters, who from eternity doth teach
Himself in all, and all things in himself.
Great universal Teacher! he shall mould
Thy spirit, and by giving make it ask.

   Therefore all seasons shall be sweet to thee,   65
Whether the summer clothe the general earth
With greenness, or the redbreast sit and sing
Betwixt the tufts of snow on the bare branch
Of mossy apple-tree, while the nigh thatch
Smokes in the sun-thaw; whether the eve-drops fall   70
Heard only in the trances of the blast,
Or if the secret ministry of frost
Shall hang them up in silent icicles,
Quietly shining to the quiet Moon.

Lewti

OR THE CIRCASSIAN LOVE-CHAUNT

At midnight by the stream I roved,
To forget the form I loved.
Image of Lewti! from my mind
Depart; for Lewti is not kind.
The Moon was high, the moonlight gleam   5
   And the shadow of a star
Heaved upon Tamaha's stream;

But the rock shone brighter far,
The rock half sheltered from my view
By pendent boughs of tressy yew—   10
So shines my Lewti's forehead fair,
Gleaming through her sable hair.
Image of Lewti! from my mind
Depart; for Lewti is not kind.

I saw a cloud of palest hue,   15
    Onward to the moon it passed;
Still brighter and more bright it grew,
With floating colours not a few,
    Till it reached the moon at last:
Then the cloud was wholly bright,   20
With a rich and amber light!
And so with many a hope I seek,
    And with such joy I find my Lewti;
And even so my pale wan cheek
    Drinks in as deep a flush of beauty!   25
Nay, treacherous image! leave my mind,
If Lewti never will be kind.

The little cloud—it floats away,
    Away it goes; away so soon?
Alas! it has no power to stay: 30
Its hues are dim, its hues are grey—
    Away it passes from the moon!
How mournfully it seems to fly,
    Ever fading more and more,
To joyless regions of the sky—   35
    And now 'tis whiter than before!
As white as my poor cheek will be,
    When, Lewti! on my couch I lie,
A dying man for love of thee.

71

Nay, treacherous image! leave my mind— 40
And yet, thou did'st not look unkind.
  I saw a vapour in the sky,
  Thin, and white, and very high;
I ne'er beheld so thin a cloud:
  Perhaps the breezes that can fly 45
  Now below and now above,
Have snatched aloft the lawny shroud
  Of Lady fair—that died for love.
For maids, as well as youths, have perished
From fruitless love too fondly cherished. 50
Nay, treacherous image! leave my mind—
For Lewti never will be kind.

Hush! my heedless feet from under
  Slip the crumbling banks for ever:
Like echoes to a distant thunder, 55
  They plunge into the gentle river.
The river-swans have heard my tread,
And startle from their reedy bed.
O beauteous birds! methinks ye measure
  Your movements to some heavenly tune! 60
O beauteous birds! 'tis such a pleasure
  To see you move beneath the moon,
I would it were your true delight
To sleep by day and wake all night.
I know the place where Lewti lies, 65
When silent night has closed her eyes:
  It is a breezy jasmine-bower,
The nightingale sings o'er her head:
  Voice of the night! had I the power
That leafy labyrinth to thread, 70
And creep, like thee, with soundless tread,

I then might view her bosom white
Heaving lovely to my sight,
As these two swans together heave
On the gently swelling wave.   75

Oh! that she saw me in a dream,
    And dreamt that I had died for care;
All pale and wasted I would seem,
    Yet fair withal, as spirits are!
I'd die indeed, if I might see   80
Her bosom heave, and heave for me!
Soothe, gentle image! soothe my mind!
To-morrow Lewti may be kind.

Fears in Solitude

WRITTEN IN APRIL, 1798, DURING THE ALARM OF
AN INVASION

A green and silent spot, amid the hills,
A small and silent dell! O'er stiller place
No singing sky-lark ever poised himself.
The hills are heathy, save that swelling slope,
Which hath a gay and gorgeous covering on,   5
All golden with the never-bloomless furze,
Which now blooms most profusely: but the dell,
Bathed by the mist, is fresh and delicate
As vernal corn-field, or the unripe flax,
When, through its half-transparent stalks, at eve,   10
The level sunshine glimmers with green light.
Oh! 'tis a quiet spirit-healing nook!
Which all, methinks, would love; but chiefly he,

The humble man, who, in his youthful years,
Knew just so much of folly, as had made   15
His early manhood more securely wise!
Here he might lie on fern or withered heath,
While from the singing-lark (that sings unseen
The minstrelsy that solitude loves best,)
And from the sun, and from the breezy air,   20
Sweet influences trembled o'er his frame;
And he, with many feelings, many thoughts,
Made up a meditative joy, and found
Religious meanings in the forms of nature!
And so, his sense gradually wrapt   25
In a half sleep, he dreams of better worlds,
And dreaming hears thee still, O singing-lark;
That singest like an angel in the clouds!

   My God! it is a melancholy thing
For such a man, who would full fain preserve   30
His soul in calmness, yet perforce must feel
For all his human brethren—O my God!
It weighs upon the heart, that he must think
What uproar and what strife may now be stirring
This way or that way o'er these silent hills—   35
Invasion, and the thunder and the shout,
And all the crash of onset; fear and rage,
And undetermined conflict—even now,
Even now, perchance, and in his native isle:
Carnage and groans beneath this blessed sun!   40
We have offended, Oh! my countrymen!
We have offended very grievously,
And been most tyrannous. From east to west
A groan of accusation pierces Heaven!
The wretched plead against us; multitudes   45
Countless and vehement, the sons of God,

Our brethren! Like a cloud that travels on,
Steamed up from Cairo's swamps of pestilence,
Even so, my countrymen! have we gone forth
And borne to distant tribes slavery and pangs,   50
And, deadlier far, our vices, whose deep taint
With slow perdition murders the whole man,
His body and his soul! Meanwhile, at home,
All individual dignity and power
Engulfed in courts, committees, institutions,   55
Associations and societies,
A vain, speech-mouthing, speech-reporting guild,
One benefit-club for mutual flattery.
We have drunk up, demure as at a grace,
Pollutions from the brimming cup of wealth;   60
Contemptuous of all honourable rule,
Yet bartering freedom and the poor man's life
For gold, as at a market! The sweet words
Of Christian promise, words that even yet
Might stem destruction, were they wisely preached,   65
Are muttered o'er by men, whose tones proclaim
How flat and wearisome they feel their trade:
Rank scoffers some, but most too indolent
To deem them falsehoods or to know their truth.
Oh! blasphemous! the book of life is made
A superstitious instrument, on which   70
We gabble o'er the oaths we mean to break;
For all must swear—all and in every place,
College and wharf, council and justice-court;
All, all must swear, the briber and the bribed,
Merchant and lawyer, senator and priest,   75
The rich, the poor, the old man and the young;
All, all make up one scheme of perjury,
That faith doth reel; the very name of God
Sounds like a juggler's charm; and, bold with joy,

Forth from his dark and lonely hiding-place,
(Portentous sight!) the owlet Atheism,
Sailing on obscene wings athwart the noon,
Drops his blue-fringed lids, and holds them close,
And hooting at the glorious sun in Heaven,   85
Cries out, 'Where is it?'

                              Thankless too for peace,
(Peace long preserved by fleets and perilous seas)
Secure from actual warfare, we have loved
To swell the war-whoop, passionate for war!
Alas! for ages ignorant of all   90
Its ghastlier workings, (famine or blue plague,
Battle, or siege, or flight through wintry snows,)
We, this whole people, have been clamorous
For war and bloodshed; animating sports,
The which we pay for as a thing to talk of,   95
Spectators and not combatants! No guess
Anticipative of a wrong unfelt,
No speculation on contingency,
However dim and vague, too vague and dim
To yield a justifying cause; and forth,   100
(Stuffed out with big preamble, holy names,
And adjurations of the God in Heaven,)
We send our mandates for the certain death
Of thousands and ten thousands! Boys and girls,
And women, that would groan to see a child   105
Pull off an insect's leg, all read of war,
The best amusement for our morning-meal!
The poor wretch, who has learnt his only prayers
From curses, who knows scarcely words enough
To ask a blessing from his Heavenly Father,   110
Becomes a fluent phraseman, absolute
And technical in victories and defeats,

And all our dainty terms for fratricide;
Terms which we trundle smoothly o'er our tongues
Like mere abstractions, empty sounds to which   115
We join no feeling and attach no form!
As if the soldier died without a wound;
As if the fibres of this godlike frame
Were gored without a pang; as if the wretch
Who fell in battle, doing bloody deeds,   120
Passed off to Heaven, translated and not killed;
As though he had no wife to pine for him,
No God to judge him! Therefore, evil days
Are coming on us, O my countrymen!
And what if all-avenging Providence,   125
Strong and retributive, should make us know
The meaning of our words, force us to feel
The desolation and the agony
Of our fierce doings!
               Spare us yet awhile,
Father and God! O! spare us yet awhile!   130
Oh! let not English women drag their flight
Fainting beneath the burthen of their babes,
Of the sweet infants, that but yesterday
Laughed at the breast! Sons, brothers, husbands, all
Who ever gazed with fondness on the forms   135
Which grew up with you round the same fire-side,
And all who ever heard the sabbath-bells
Without the infidel's scorn, make yourselves pure!
Stand forth! be men! repel an impious foe,
Impious and false, a light yet cruel race,   140
Who laugh away all virtue, mingling mirth
With deeds of murder; and still promising
Freedom, themselves too sensual to be free,
Poison life's amities, and cheat the heart
Of faith and quiet hope, and all that soothes   145

And all that lifts the spirit! Stand we forth;
Render them back upon the insulted ocean,
And let them toss as idly on its waves
As the vile sea-weed, which some mountain-blast
Swept from our shores! And oh! may we return   150
Not with a drunken triumph, but with fear,
Repenting of the wrongs with which we stung
So fierce a foe to frenzy!

                    I have told,
O Britons! O my brethren! I have told
Most bitter truth, but without bitterness.   155
Nor deem my zeal or factious or mis-timed;
For never can true courage dwell with them,
Who, playing tricks with conscience, dare not look
At their own vices. We have been too long
Dupes of a deep delusion! Some, belike,   160
Groaning with restless enmity, expect
All change from change of constituted power;
As if a Government had been a robe,
On which our vice and wretchedness were tagged
Like fancy-points and fringes, with the robe   165
Pulled off at pleasure. Fondly these attach
A radical causation to a few
Poor drudges of chastising Providence,
Who borrow all their hues and qualities
From our own folly and rank wickedness,   170
Which gave them birth and nursed them. Others, mean-
    while,
Dote with a mad idolatry; and all
Who will not fall before their images,
And yield them worship, they are enemies
Even of their country!

                              Such have I been deemed—   175
But, O dear Britain! O my Mother Isle!
Needs must thou prove a name most dear and holy
To me, a son, a brother, and a friend,
A husband, and a father! who revere
All bonds of natural love, and find them all   180
Within the limits of thy rocky shores.
O native Britain! O my Mother Isle!
How shouldst thou prove aught else but dear and holy
To me, who from thy lakes and mountain-hills,
Thy clouds, thy quiet dales, thy rocks and seas,   185
Have drunk in all my intellectual life,
All sweet sensations, all ennobling thoughts,
All adoration of the God in nature,
All lovely and all honourable things,
Whatever makes this mortal spirit feel   190
The joy and greatness of its future being?
There lives nor form nor feeling in my soul
Unborrowed from my country. O divine
And beauteous island! thou hast been my sole
And most magnificent temple, in the which   195
I walk with awe, and sing my stately songs,
Loving the God that made me!

                              May my fears,
My filial fears, be vain! and may the vaunts
And menace of the vengeful enemy
Pass like the gust, that roared and died away   200
In the distant tree: which heard, and only heard
In this low dell, bowed not the delicate grass.

  But now the gentle dew-fall sends abroad
The fruit-like perfume of the golden furze:

The light has left the summit of the hill,   205
Though still a sunny gleam lies beautiful,
Aslant the ivied beacon. Now farewell,
Farewell, awhile, O soft and silent spot!
On the green sheep-track, up the heathy hill,
Homeward I wind my way; and lo! recalled   210
From bodings that have well nigh wearied me,
I find myself upon the brow, and pause
Startled! And after lonely sojourning
In such a quiet and surrounded nook,
This burst of prospect, here the shadowy main,   215
Dim tinted, there the mighty majesty
Of that huge amphitheatre of rich
And elmy fields, seems like society—
Conversing with the mind, and giving it
A livelier impulse and a dance of thought!   220
And now, beloved Stowey! I behold
Thy church-tower, and, methinks, the four huge elms
Clustering, which mark the mansion of my friend;
And close behind them, hidden from my view,
Is my own lowly cottage, where my babe   225
And my babe's mother dwell in peace! With light
And quickened footsteps thitherward I tend,
Remembering thee, O green and silent dell!
And grateful, that by nature's quietness
And solitary musings, all my heart   230
Is softened, and made worthy to indulge
Love, and the thoughts that yearn for human kind.

The Nightingale

A CONVERSATION POEM. APRIL 1798

No cloud, no relique of the sunken day
Distinguishes the West, no long thin slip
Of sullen light, no obscure trembling hues.
Come, we will rest on this old mossy bridge!
You see the glimmer of the stream beneath,   5
But hear no murmuring: it flows silently,
O'er its soft bed of verdure. All is still,
A balmy night! and though the stars be dim,
Yet let us think upon the vernal showers
That gladden the green earth, and we shall find   10
A pleasure in the dimness of the stars.
And hark! the Nightingale begins its song,
'Most musical, most melancholy' bird![1]
A melancholy bird! Oh! idle thought!
In nature there is nothing melancholy.   15
But some night-wandering man whose heart was pierced
With the remembrance of a grievous wrong,
Or slow distemper, or neglected love,
(And so, poor wretch! filled all things with himself,
And made all gentle sounds tell back the tale   20
Of his own sorrow) he, and such as he,
First named these notes a melancholy strain.

[1] *'Most musical, most melancholy.'* This passage in Milton possesses an excellence far superior to that of mere description. It is spoken in the character of the melancholy man, and has therefore a dramatic propriety. The author makes this remark, to rescue himself from the charge of having alluded with levity, to a line in Milton.

And many a poet echoes the conceit;
Poet who hath been building up the rhyme
When he had better far have stretched his limbs   25
Beside a brook in mossy forest-dell,
By sun or moon-light, to the influxes
Of shapes and sounds and shifting elements
Surrendering his whole spirit, of his song
And of his fame forgetful! so his fame   30
Should share in Nature's immortality,
A venerable thing! and so his song
Should make all Nature lovelier, and itself
Be loved like Nature! But 'twill not be so;
And youths and maidens most poetical,   35
Who lost the deepening twilights of the spring
In ball-rooms and hot theatres, they still
Full of meek sympathy must heave their sighs
O'er Philomela's pity-pleading strains.

   My Friend, and thou, our Sister! we have learnt   40
A different lore: we may not thus profane
Nature's sweet voices, always full of love
And joyance! 'Tis the merry Nightingale
That crowds, and hurries, and precipitates
With fast thick warble his delicious notes,   45
As he were fearful that an April night
Would be too short for him to utter forth
His love-chant, and disburthen his full soul
Of all its music!

                         And I know a grove
Of large extent, hard by a castle huge,   50
Which the great lord inhabits not; and so
This grove is wild with tangling underwood,

And the trim walks are broken up, and grass,
Thin grass and king-cups grow within the paths.
But never elsewhere in one place I knew   55
So many nightingales; and far and near,
In wood and thicket, over the wide grove,
They answer and provoke each other's song,
With skirmish and capricious passagings,
And murmurs musical and swift jug jug,   60
And one low piping sound more sweet than all—
Stirring the air with such a harmony,
That should you close your eyes, you might almost
Forget it was not day! On moon-lit bushes,
Whose dewy leaflets are but half disclosed,   65
You may perchance behold them on the twigs,
Their bright, bright eyes, their eyes both bright and full,
Glistening, while many a glow-worm in the shade
Lights up her love-torch.

                A most gentle Maid,
Who dwelleth in her hospitable home   70
Hard by the castle, and at latest eve
(Even like a Lady vowed and dedicate
To something more than Nature in the grove)
Glides through the pathways; she knows all their notes,
That gentle Maid! and oft a moment's space,   75
What time the moon was lost behind a cloud,
Hath heard a pause of silence; till the moon
Emerging, hath awakened earth and sky
With one sensation, and these wakeful birds
Have all burst forth in choral minstrelsy,   80
As if some sudden gale had swept at once
A hundred airy harps! And she hath watched
Many a nightingale perched giddily
On blossomy twig still swinging from the breeze,

And to that motion tune his wanton song   85
Like tipsy joy that reels with tossing head.

  Farewell, O Warbler! till to-morrow eve,
And you, my friends! farewell, a short farewell!
We have been loitering long and pleasantly,
And now for our dear homes.—That strain again!   90
Full fain it would delay me! My dear babe,
Who, capable of no articulate sound,
Mars all things with his imitative lisp,
How he would place his hand beside his ear,
His little hand, the small forefinger up,   95
And bid us listen! And I deem it wise
To make him Nature's play-mate. He knows well
The evening-star; and once, when he awoke
In most distressful mood (some inward pain
Had made up that strange thing, an infant's dream.—) 100
I hurried with him to our orchard-plot,
And he beheld the moon, and, hushed at once,
Suspends his sobs, and laughs most silently,
While his fair eyes, that swam with undropped tears,
Did glitter in the yellow moon-beam! Well!—   105
It is a father's tale: But if that Heaven
Should give me life, his childhood shall grow up
Familiar with these songs, that with the night
He may associate joy.—Once more, farewell,
Sweet Nightingale! Once more, my friends! farewell.   110

Kubla Khan

In Xanadu did Kubla Khan
A stately pleasure-dome decree:
Where Alph, the sacred river, ran
Through caverns measureless to man
  Down to a sunless sea. 5
So twice five miles of fertile ground
With walls and towers were girdled round:
And there were gardens bright with sinuous rills
Where blossomed many an incense-bearing tree;
And here were forests ancient as the hills, 10
Enfolding sunny spots of greenery.

But oh! that deep romantic chasm which slanted
Down the green hill athwart a cedarn cover!
A savage place! as holy and enchanted
As e'er beneath a waning moon was haunted 15
By woman wailing for her demon-lover!
And from this chasm, with ceaseless turmoil seething,
As if this earth in fast thick pants were breathing,
A mighty fountain momently was forced:
Amid whose swift half-intermitted burst 20
Huge fragments vaulted like rebounding hail,
Or chaffy grain beneath the thresher's flail:
And mid these dancing rocks at once and ever
It flung up momently the sacred river.
Five miles meandering with a mazy motion 25
Through wood and dale the sacred river ran,

Then reached the caverns measureless to man,
And sank in tumult to a lifeless ocean:
And 'mid this tumult Kubla heard from far
Ancestral voices prophesying war!   30

    The shadow of the dome of pleasure
    Floated midway on the waves;
    Where was heard the mingled measure
    From the fountain and the caves.
It was a miracle of rare device,   35
A sunny pleasure-dome with caves of ice!

    A damsel with a dulcimer
    In a vision once I saw:
    It was an Abyssinian maid,
    And on her dulcimer she played,   40
    Singing of Mount Abora.
    Could I revive within me
    Her symphony and song,
    To such a deep delight 'twould win me
That with music loud and long,   45
I would build that dome in air,
That sunny dome! those caves of ice!
And all who heard should see them there,
And all should cry, Beware! Beware!
His flashing eyes, his floating hair!   50
Weave a circle round him thrice,
And close your eyes with holy dread,
For he on honey-dew hath fed,
And drunk the milk of Paradise.

Love

All thoughts, all passions, all delights,
Whatever stirs this mortal frame,
All are but ministers of Love,
    And feed his sacred flame.

Oft in my waking dreams do I   5
Live o'er again that happy hour,
When midway on the mount I lay,
    Beside the ruined tower.

The moonshine, stealing o'er the scene
Had blended with the lights of eve;   10
And she was there, my hope, my joy,
    My own dear Genevieve!

She lean'd against the armed man,
The statue of the armed knight;
She stood and listened to my lay,   15
    Amid the lingering light.

Few sorrows hath she of her own,
My hope! my joy! my Genevieve!
She loves me best, whene'er I sing
    The songs that make her grieve.   20

I played a soft and doleful air,
I sang an old and moving story—
An old rude song, that suited well
    That ruin wild and hoary.

She listened with a flitting blush, 25
With downcast eyes and modest grace;
For well she knew, I could not choose
 But gaze upon her face.

I told her of the Knight that wore
Upon his shield a burning brand; 30
And that for ten long years he wooed
 The Lady of the Land.

I told her how he pined: and ah!
The deep, the low, the pleading tone
With which I sang another's love, 35
 Interpreted my own.

She listened with a flitting blush,
With downcast eyes, and modest grace;
And she forgave me, that I gazed
 Too fondly on her face! 40

But when I told the cruel scorn
That crazed that bold and lovely Knight,
And that he crossed the mountain-woods,
 Nor rested day nor night;

That sometimes from the savage den, 45
And sometimes from the darksome shade,
And sometimes starting up at once
 In green and sunny glade,—

There came and looked him in the face
An angel beautiful and bright; 50
And that he knew it was a Fiend,
 This miserable Knight!

And that unknowing what he did,
He leaped amid a murderous band,
And saved from outrage worse than death 55
  The Lady of the Land;—

And how she wept, and clasped his knees;
And how she tended him in vain—
And ever strove to expiate
  The scorn that crazed his brain;— 60

And that she nursed him in a cave;
And how his madness went away,
When on the yellow forest-leaves
  A dying man he lay;—

His dying words—but when I reached 65
That tenderest strain of all the ditty,
My faltering voice and pausing harp
  Disturbed her soul with pity!

All impulses of soul and sense
Had thrilled my guileless Genevieve; 70
The music and the doleful tale,
  The rich and balmy eve;

And hopes, and fears that kindle hope,
An indistinguishable throng,
And gentle wishes long subdued, 75
  Subdued and cherished long!

She wept with pity and delight,
She blushed with love, and virgin shame;
And like the murmur of a dream,
  I heard her breathe my name. 80

Her bosom heaved—she stepped aside,
As conscious of my look she stept—
Then suddenly, with timorous eye
    She fled to me and wept.

She half inclosed me with her arms,   85
She pressed me with a meek embrace;
And bending back her head, looked up,
    And gazed upon my face.

'Twas partly love, and partly fear,
And partly 'twas a bashful art,   90
That I might rather feel, than see,
    The swelling of her heart.

I calmed her fears, and she was calm,
And told her love with virgin pride;
And so I won my Genevieve,   95
    My bright and beauteous Bride.

The Keepsake

The tedded hay, the first fruits of the soil,
The tedded hay and corn-sheaves in one field,
Show summer gone, ere come. The foxglove tall
Sheds its loose purple bells, or in the gust,
Or when it bends beneath the up-springing lark,   5
Or mountain-finch alighting. And the rose
(In vain the darling of successful love)
Stands, like some boasted beauty of past years,
The thorns remaining, and the flowers all gone.

Nor can I find, amid my lonely walk   10
By rivulet, or spring, or wet road-side,
That blue and bright-eyed floweret of the brook,
Hope's gentle gem, the sweet Forget-me-not!
So will not fade the flowers which Emmeline
With delicate fingers on the snow-white silk   15
Has worked, (the flowers which most she knew I loved,)
And, more beloved than they, her auburn hair.

  In the cool morning twilight, early waked
By her full bosom's joyous restlessness,
Softly she rose, and lightly stole along,   20
Down the slope coppice to the woodbine bower,
Whose rich flowers, swinging in the morning breeze,
Over their dim fast-moving shadows hung,
Making a quiet image of disquiet
In the smooth, scarcely moving river-pool.   25
There, in that bower where first she owned her love,
And let me kiss my own warm tear of joy
From off her glowing cheek, she sate and stretched
The silk upon the frame, and worked her name
Between the Moss-Rose and Forget-me-not—   30
Her own dear name, with her own auburn hair!
That forced to wander till sweet spring return,
I yet might ne'er forget her smile, her look,
Her voice, (that even in her mirthful mood
Has made me wish to steal away and weep,)   35
Nor yet the entrancement of that maiden kiss
With which she promised, that when spring returned,
She would resign one half of that dear name,
And own henceforth no other name but mine!

Ode to Tranquillity

Tranquillity! thou better name
Than all the family of Fame!
Thou ne'er wilt leave my riper age
To low intrigue, or factious rage;
For oh! dear child of thoughtful Truth,   5
To thee I gave my early youth,
And left the bark, and blest the steadfast shore,
Ere yet the tempest rose and scared me with its roar.

Who late and lingering seeks thy shrine,
On him but seldom, Power divine,   10
Thy spirit rests! Satiety
And Sloth, poor counterfeits of thee,
Mock the tired worldling. Idle hope
And dire remembrance interlope,
To vex the feverish slumbers of the mind: 15
The bubble floats before, the spectre stalks behind.

But me thy gentle hand will lead
At morning through the accustomed mead;
And in the sultry summer's heat
Will build me up a mossy seat;   20
And when the gust of Autumn crowds,
And breaks the busy moon-light clouds,
Thou best the thought canst raise, the heart attune,
Light as the busy clouds, calm as the gliding moon.

The feeling heart, the searching soul,   25
To thee I dedicate the whole!

And while within myself I trace
The greatness of some future race,
Aloof with hermit-eye I scan
The present works of present man—   30
  A wild and dream-like trade of blood and guile,
  Too foolish for a tear, too wicked for a smile!

To Asra

Are there two things, of all which men possess,
That are so like each other and so near,
As mutual Love seems like to Happiness?
Dear Asra, woman beyond utterance dear!
This Love which ever welling at my heart,   5
Now in its living fount doth heave and fall,
Now overflowing pours thro' every part
Of all my frame, and fills and changes all,
Like vernal waters springing up through snow,
This Love that seeming great beyond the power   10
Of growth, yet seemeth ever more to grow,
Could I transmute the whole to one rich Dower
Of Happy Life, and give it all to Thee,
Thy lot, methinks, were Heaven, thy age, Eternity!

Love's Sanctuary

This yearning heart (Love! witness what I say)
Enshrines thy form as purely as it may,
Round which, as to some spirit uttering bliss,
My thoughts all stand ministrant night and day
Like saintly Priests, that dare not think amiss.

Dejection

A LETTER

Well! if the Bard was weatherwise, who made
The grand old Ballad of Sir Patrick Spence,
This Night, so tranquil now, will not go hence
Unrous'd by winds, that ply a busier trade
Than that, which moulds yon clouds in lazy flakes, 5
Or the dull sobbing Draft, that drones and rakes
Upon the Strings of this Eolian Lute,
Which better far were mute.
For, lo! the New Moon, winter-bright!
And overspread with phantom Light 10
(With swimming phantom Light o'erspread
But rimm'd and circled with a silver Thread)
I see the Old Moon in her Lap, foretelling
The coming-on of Rain and squally Blast—
O! Sara! that the Gust ev'n now were swelling, 15
And the slant Night-shower driving loud and fast!

A Grief without a pang, void, dark and drear,
A stifling, drowsy, unimpassion'd Grief
That finds no natural outlet, no Relief
In word, or sigh, or tear— 20
This, Sara! well though know'st,
Is that sore Evil, which I dread the most,
And oft'nest suffer! In this heartless Mood,
To other thoughts by yonder Throstle woo'd,
That pipes within the Larch tree, not unseen, 25
(The Larch, which pushes out in tassels green

94

It's bundled Leafits) woo'd to mild Delights
By all the tender Sounds and gentle Sights
Of this sweet Primrose-month—and *vainly* woo'd
O dearest Sara! in this heartless Mood   30
All this long Eve, so balmy and serene,
Have I been gazing on the western Sky
And its peculiar Tint of Yellow Green—
And still I gaze—and with how blank an eye!
And those thin Clouds above, in flakes and bars,   35
That give away their Motion to the Stars;
Those Stars, that glide behind them, or between,
Now sparkling, now bedimm'd, but always seen;
Yon crescent Moon, as fix'd as if it grew
In it's own cloudless, starless Lake of Blue—   40
A boat becalm'd! dear William's Sky Canoe!
—I see them all, so excellently fair!
I see, not feel, how beautiful they are.

My genial Spirits fail—
And what can these avail   45
To lift the smoth'ring Weight from off my Breast?
It were a vain Endeavor,
Tho' I should gaze for ever
On that Green Light that lingers in the West!
I may not hope from outward Forms to win   50
The Passion and the Life, whose Fountains are within!

These lifeless Shapes, around, below, Above,
    O what can they impart?
When even the gentle Thought, that thou, my Love!
Art gazing, now, like me,   55
And see'st the Heaven, I see—
Sweet Thought it is—yet feebly stirs my Heart!

Feebly! O feebly!—Yet
(I well remember it)
In my first Dawn of Youth that Fancy stole   60
With many secret Yearnings on my Soul.
At eve, sky-gazing in 'ecstatic fit'
(Alas! for cloister'd in a city School
The Sky was all, I knew, of Beautiful)
At the barr'd window often did I sit,   65
And oft upon the leaded School-roof lay,
And to myself would say—
There does not live the Man so stripp'd of good affections
As not to love to see a Maiden's quiet Eyes
Uprais'd, and linking on sweet Dreams by dim Connections 70
To Moon, or Evening Star, or glorious western Skies—
While yet a Boy, this Thought would so pursue me,
That often it became a kind of Vision to me!

Sweet Thought! and dear of old
To Hearts of finer Mould!   75
Ten thousand times by Friends and Lovers blest!
I spake with rash Despair,
And ere I was aware,
The Weight was somewhat lifted from my Breast!
O Sara! in the weather-fended Wood,   80
Thy lov'd haunt! where the Stock-doves coo at Noon
I guess, that thou hast stood
And watch'd yon Crescent, and it's ghost-like Moon.
And yet, far rather in my present Mood
I would, that thou'dst been sitting all this while   85
Upon the sod-built Seat of Camomile—
And tho' thy Robin may have ceas'd to sing,
Yet needs for *my* sake must thou love to hear
The Bee-hive murmuring near,

That ever-busy and most quiet Thing   90
Which I have heard at Midnight murmuring.

I feel my spirit moved.
And whereso'er thou be,
O Sister! O Beloved!
Those dear mild Eyes, that see   95
Even now the Heaven, *I* see—
There is a Prayer in them! It is for *me*—
And I, dear Sara, *I* am blessing *thee*!

It was as calm as this, that happy night
When Mary, thou, and I together were,   100
The low decaying Fire our only Light,
And listen'd to the Stillness of the Air!
O that affectionate and blameless Maid,
Dear Mary! on her Lap my head she lay'd—
Her Hand was on my Brow,   105
Even as my own is now;
And on my Cheek I felt the eye-lash play.
Such joy I had, that I may truly say,
My spirit was awe-stricken with the Excess
And trance-like Depth of it's brief Happiness.   110

Ah fair Remembrances, that so revive
The Heart, and fill it with a living Power,
Where were they, Sara?—or did I not strive
To win them to me?—on the fretting Hour
Then when I wrote thee that complaining Scroll,   115
Which even to bodily Sickness bruis'd thy Soul!
And yet thou blam'st thyself alone! And yet
Forbidd'st me all Regret!

And must I not regret, that I distress'd
Thee, best belov'd, who lovest me the best?   120
My better mind had fled, I know not whither,
For O! was this an absent Friend's Employ
To send from far both Pain and Sorrow thither
Where still his Blessings should have call'd down Joy!
I read thy guileless Letter o'er again—   125
I hear thee of thy blameless Self complain—
And only this I learn—and this, alas! I know—
That thou art weak and pale with Sickness, Grief, and Pain—
And *I*,—*I* made thee so!

O for my own sake I regret perforce   130
Whatever turns thee, Sara! from the course
Of calm Well-being and a Heart at rest!
When thou, and with thee those, whom thou lov'st best,
Shall dwell together in one happy Home,
One House, the dear *abiding* Home of All,   135
I too will crown me with a Coronal—
Nor shall this Heart in idle Wishes roam
        Morbidly soft!
No! let me trust, that I shall wear away
In no inglorious Toils the manly Day,   140
And only now and then, and not too oft,
Some dear and memorable Eve will bless
Dreaming of all your Loves and Quietness.
Be happy, and I need thee not in sight.
Peace in thy Heart, and Quiet in thy Dwelling,   145
Health in thy Limbs, and in thine eyes the Light
Of Love and Hope and honorable Feeling—
Where e'er I am, I shall be well content!
Not near thee, haply shall be more content!
To all things I prefer the Permanent.   150
And better seems it, for a Heart, like mine,

Always to *know*, than sometimes to behold,
   Their Happiness and thine—
For Change doth trouble me with pangs untold!
To see thee, hear thee, feel thee—then to part   150
   Oh! it weighs down the heart!
To *visit* those, I love, as I love thee,
Mary, and William, and dear Dorothy,
It is but a temptation to repine—
The transientness is Poison in the Wine,   160
Eats out the pith of Joy, makes all Joy hollow,
All Pleasure a dim Dream of Pain to follow!
My own peculiar Lot, my house-hold Life
It is, and will remain, Indifference or Strife.
While *Ye* are *well* and *happy*, 'twould but wrong you   165
If I should fondly yearn to be among you—
Wherefore, O wherefore! should I wish to be
A wither'd branch upon a blossoming Tree?

But (let me say it! for I vainly strive
To beat away the Thought), but if thou pin'd   170
Whate'er the Cause, in body or in mind,
I were the miserablest Man alive
To know it and be absent! Thy Delights
Far off, or near, alike I may partake—
But O! to mourn for thee, and to forsake   175
All power, all hope, of giving comfort to thee—
To know that thou art weak and worn with pain,
And not to hear thee, Sara! not to view thee—
   Not sit beside thy Bed,
   Not press thy aching Head,   180
   Not bring thee Health again—
   At least to hope, to try—
By this Voice, which thou lov'st, and by this earnest Eye—
Nay, wherefore did I let it haunt my Mind

The dark distressful Dream!   185
I turn from it, and listen to the Wind
Which long has rav'd unnotic'd! What a Scream
Of agony, by Torture lengthen'd out
That Lute sent forth! O thou wild Storm without!
Jagg'd Rock, or mountain Pond, or blasted Tree,   190
Or Pine-Grove, whither Woodman never clomb,
Or lonely House, long held the Witches' Home,
Methinks were fitter Instruments for Thee,
Mad Lutanist! that in this month of Showers,
Of dark brown Gardens and of peeping Flowers,   195
Mak'st Devil's Yule with worse than wintry Song
The Blossoms, Buds, and timorous Leaves among!
Thou Actor, perfect in all tragic Sounds!
Thou mighty Poet, even to frenzy bold!
What tell'st thou now about?   200
'Tis of the Rushing of an Host in Rout
And many groans for men with smarting Wounds—
At once they groan with smart, and shudder with the cold!
'Tis hush'd! there is a Trance of deepest Silence,
Again! but all that Sound, as of a rushing Crowd,   205
And Groans and tremulous Shudderings, all are over.
And it has other Sounds, and all less deep, less loud!
A Tale of less Affright,
And tempered with Delight,
As William's self had made the tender Lay—   210
'Tis of a little Child
Upon a heathy Wild,
Not far from home, but it has lost it's way—
And now moans low in utter grief and fear—
And now screams loud, and hopes to make it's Mother hear!

'Tis Midnight! and small Thoughts have I of Sleep.   216
Full seldom may my Friend such Vigils keep—

O breathe She softly in her gentle Sleep!
Cover her, gentle sleep! with wings of Healing.
And be this Tempest but a Mountain Birth! 220
May all the Stars hang bright above her Dwelling,
Silent, as though they *watch'd* the sleeping Earth!
Healthful and light, my Darling! may'st thou rise
With clear and chearful Eyes—
And of the same good Tidings to me send! 225
For oh! beloved Friend!
I am not the buoyant Thing I was of yore
When like an own Child, I to Joy belong'd:
For others mourning oft, myself oft sorely wrong'd,
Yet bearing all things then, as if I nothing bore! 230

Yes, dearest Sara, yes!
There *was* a time when tho' my path was rough,
The Joy within me dallied with Distress;
And all Misfortunes were but as the Stuff
Whence Fancy made me Dreams of Happiness; 235
For Hope grew round me, like the climbing Vine,
And Leaves and Fruitage, not my own, seem'd mine!
But now Ill Tidings bow me down to earth,
Nor care I that they rob me of my Mirth—
But Oh! each Visitation 240
Suspends what nature gave me at my Birth,
My shaping spirit of Imagination!

I speak not now of those habitual Ills
That wear out Life, when two unequal Minds
Meet in one House and two discordant Wills— 245
    This leaves me, where it finds,
Past Cure, and past Complaint,—a fate austere
Too fix'd and hopeless to partake of Fear!

But thou, dear Sara! (dear indeed thou art,
My Comforter, a Heart within my Heart!)   250
Thou, and the Few, we love, tho' few ye be,
Make up a World of Hopes and Fears for me.
And if Affliction, or distemp'ring Pain,
Or wayward Chance befall you, I complain
Not that I mourn—O Friends, most dear! most true!   255
  Methinks to weep with you
Were better far than to rejoice alone—
But that my coarse domestic Life has known
No Habits of heart-nursing Sympathy,
No Griefs but such as dull and deaden me,   260
No mutual mild Enjoyments of it's own,
No Hopes of its own Vintage, None O! none—
Whence when I mourn'd for you, my Heart might borrow
Fair forms and living Motions for it's Sorrow.
For not to think of what I needs must feel,   265
But to be still and patient all I can;
And haply by abstruse Research to steal
From my own Nature, all the Natural man—
This was my sole Resource, my wisest plan!
And that, which suits a part, infects the whole,   270
And now is almost grown the Temper of my Soul.

My little Children are a Joy, a Love,
  A good Gift from above!
But what is Bliss, that still calls up a Woe,
  And makes it doubly keen   275
Compelling me to *feel,* as well as *know,*
What a most blessed Lot mine might have been.
Those little Angel Children (woe is me!)
There have been hours when feeling how they bind
And pluck out the Wing-feathers of my Mind,   280

Turning my Error to Necessity,
I have half-wish'd they never had been born!
That seldom! but sad Thoughts they always bring,
And like the Poet's Philomel, I sing
My Love-song, with my breast against a Thorn.   285

With no unthankful Spirit I confess,
This clinging Grief, too, in it's turn, awakes
That Love, and Father's Joy; but O! it makes
The Love the greater, and the Joy far less.
These Mountains too, these Vales, these Woods, these Lakes,
Scenes full of Beauty and of Loftiness   291
Where all my Life I fondly hop'd to live—
I were sunk low indeed, did they *no* solace give;
But oft I seem to feel, and evermore I fear,
They are not to me now the Things, which once they were.

O Sara! we receive but what we give,   296
And in *our* life alone does Nature live
Our's is her Wedding Garment, our's her Shroud—
And would we aught behold of higher Worth
Than that inanimate cold World allow'd   300
To that poor loveless ever anxious Crowd,
Ah! from the Soul itself must issue forth
A Light, a Glory, and a luminous Cloud
Enveloping the Earth!
And from the Soul itself must there be sent   305
A sweet and potent Voice, of it's own Birth,
Of all sweet Sounds, the Life and Element.
O pure of Heart! thou need'st not ask of me
What this strong music in the Soul may be,
What and wherin it doth exist,   310
This Light, this Glory, this fair luminous Mist,

103

This beautiful and beauty-making Power!
Joy, innocent Sara! Joy, that ne'er was given
Save to the pure, and in their purest Hour,
Joy, Sara! is the Spirit and the Power,   315
That wedding Nature to us gives in Dower
      A new Earth and new Heaven,
Undreamt of by the Sensual and the Proud!
Joy is that strong Voice, Joy that luminous Cloud—
      We, we ourselves rejoice!   320
And thence flows all that charms or ear or sight,
All melodies, the Echoes of that Voice,
All Colors a Suffusion of that Light.
Sister and Friend of my devoutest Choice
Thou being innocent and full of love,   325
And nested with the Darlings of thy Love,
And feeling in thy Soul, Heart, Lips, and Arms
Even what the conjugal and mother Dove,
That borrows genial Warmth from those, she warms,
Feels in the thrill'd wings, blessedly outspread—   330
Thou free'd awhile from Cares and human Dread
By the Immenseness of the Good and Fair
    Which thou seest everywhere—
Thus, thus, should'st thou rejoice!
To thee would all things live from Pole to Pole;   335
Their Life the Eddying of thy living Soul—
O dear! O Innocent! O full of Love!
A very Friend! A Sister of my Choice—
O dear, as Light and Impulse from above,
Thus may'st thou ever, evermore rejoice!   340

The Picture

Through weeds and thorns, and matted underwood
I force my way; now climb, and now descend
O'er rocks, or bare or mossy, with wild foot
Crushing the purple whorts; while oft unseen,
Hurrying along the drifted forest-leaves,   5
The scared snake rustles. Onward still I toil
I know not, ask not whither! A new joy,
Lovely as light, sudden as summer gust,
And gladsome as the first-born of the spring,
Beckons me on, or follows from behind,   10
Playmate, or guide! The master-passion quelled,
I feel that I am free. With dun-red bark
The fir-trees, and the unfrequent slender oak,
Forth from this tangle wild of bush and brake
Soar up, and form a melancholy vault   15
High o'er me, murmuring like a distant sea.

Here Wisdom might resort, and here Remorse;
Here too the love-lorn man, who, sick in soul,
And of this busy human heart aweary,
Worships the spirit of unconscious life   20
In tree or wild-flower.—Gentle lunatic!
If so he might not wholly cease to be,
He would far rather not be that, he is;
But would be something, that he knows not of,
In winds or waters, or among the rocks!   25

Inscription

This Sycamore, oft musical with bees,—
Such tents the Patriarchs loved! O long unharmed
May all its aged boughs o'er-canopy
The small round basin, which this jutting stone
Keeps pure from falling leaves! Long may the Spring,   5
Quietly as a sleeping infant's breath,
Send up cold waters to the traveller
With soft and even pulse! Nor ever cease
Yon tiny cone of sand its soundless dance,
Which at the bottom, like a Fairy's page,   10
As merry and no taller, dances still,
Nor wrinkles the smooth surface of the Fount.
Here twilight is and coolness: here is moss,
A soft seat, and a deep and ample shade.
Thou may'st toil far and find no second tree.   15
Drink Pilgrim, here; Here rest! and if thy heart
Be innocent, here too shalt thou refresh
Thy Spirit, listening to some gentle sound,
Or passing gale or hum of murmuring bees!

A Day Dream

My eyes make pictures, when they are shut:—
    I see a fountain, large and fair,
A willow and a ruined hut,
    And thee, and me and Mary there.
O Mary! make thy gentle lap our pillow!   5
Bend o'er us, like a bower, my beautiful green willow!

A wild-rose roofs the ruined shed,
    And that and summer well agree:
And lo! where Mary leans her head,
    Two dear names carved upon the tree!   10
And Mary's tears, they are not tears of sorrow:
Our sister and our friend will both be here to-morrow.

'Twas day! But now few, large, and bright
    The stars are round the crescent moon!
And now it is a dark warm night,
    The balmiest of the month of June!   15
A glow-worm fallen, and on the marge remounting
Shines and its shadow shines, fit stars for our sweet fountain.

O ever—ever be thou blest!
    For dearly, Asra, love I thee!   20
This brooding warmth across my breast,
    This depth of tranquil bliss—ah me!
Fount, tree and shed are gone, I know not whither,
But in one quiet room we three are still together.

The shadows dance upon the wall,   25
    By the still dancing fire-flames made;
And now they slumber, moveless all!
    And now they melt to one deep shade!
But not from me shall this mild darkness steal thee:
I dream thee with mine eyes, and at my heart I feel thee! 30

Thine eyelash on my cheek doth play—
    'Tis Mary's hand upon my brow!
But let me check this tender lay
    Which none may hear but she and thou!
Like the still hive at quiet midnight humming,   35
Murmur it to yourselves, ye two beloved women

Answer to a Child's Question

Do you ask what the birds say? The sparrow, the dove,
The linnet and thrush say, 'I love and I love!'
In the winter they're silent—the wind is so strong;
What it says, I don't know, but it sings a loud song.
But green leaves, and blossoms, and sunny warm weather,
And singing, and loving—all come back together.
But the lark is so brimful of gladness and love,
The green fields below him, the blue sky above,
That he sings, and he sings; and for ever sings he—
'I love my Love, and my Love loves me!'

The Pains of Sleep

Ere on my bed my limbs I lay,
It hath not been my use to pray
With moving lips or bended knees;
But silently, by slow degrees,
My spirit I to Love compose,   5
In humble trust mine eye-lids close,
With reverential resignation,
No wish conceived, no thought exprest,
Only a sense of supplication;
A sense o'er all my soul imprest   10
That I am weak, yet not unblest,
Since in me, round me, every where
Eternal strength and wisdom are.

But yester-night I prayed aloud
In anguish and in agony,   15
Up-starting from the fiendish crowd
Of shapes and thoughts that tortured me:
A lurid light, a trampling throng,
Sense of intolerable wrong,
And whom I scorned, those only strong!   20
Thirst of revenge, the powerless will
Still baffled, and yet burning still!
Desire with loathing strangely mixed
On wild or hateful objects fixed.
Fantastic passions! maddening brawl!   25
And shame and terror over all!

Deeds to be hid which were not hid,
Which all confused I could not know,
Whether I suffered, or I did:
For all seemed guilt, remorse or woe,   30
My own or others still the same
Life-stifling fear, soul-stifling shame.

So two nights passed: the night's dismay
Saddened and stunned the coming day.
Sleep, the wide blessing, seemed to me   35
Distemper's worst calamity.
The third night, when my own loud scream
Had waked me from the fiendish dream,
O'ercome with sufferings strange and wild,
I wept as I had been a child;   40
And having thus by tears subdued
My anguish to a milder mood,
Such punishments, I said, were due
To natures deepliest stained with sin,—
For aye entempesting anew   45
The unfathomable hell within
The horror of their deeds to view,
To know and loathe, yet wish and do!
Such griefs with such men well agree,
But wherefore, wherefore fall on me?   50
To be beloved is all I need,
And whom I love, I love indeed.

Phantom

All look and likeness caught from earth,
All accident of kin and birth,
Had pass'd away. There was no trace
Of aught on that illumined face,
Uprais'd beneath the rifted stone
But of one spirit all her own;—
She, she herself, and only she,
Shone thro' her body visibly.

Constancy to an Ideal Object

Since all that beat about in Nature's range,
Or veer or vanish; why shouldst thou remain
The only constant in a world of change,
O yearning thought! that liv'st but in the brain?
Call to the hours, that in the distance play,   5
The faery people of the future day—
Fond thought! not one of all that shining swarm
Will breathe on thee with life-enkindling breath,
Till when, like strangers shelt'ring from a storm,
Hope and Despair meet in the porch of Death!   10
Yet still thou haunt'st me; and though well I see,
She is not thou, and only thou art she,
Still, still as though some dear embodied good,
Some living love before my eyes there stood
With answering look a ready ear to lend,   15
I mourn to thee and say—'Ah! loveliest friend!

That this the meed of all my toils might be,
To have a home, an English home, and thee!'
Vain repetition! Home and Thou are one.
The peacefull'st cot, the moon shall shine upon,   20
Lulled by the thrush and wakened by the lark,
Without thee were but a becalmed bark,
Whose helmsman on an ocean waste and wide
Sits mute and pale his mouldering helm beside.
And art thou nothing? Such thou art, as when   25
The woodman winding westward up the glen
At wintry dawn, where o'er the sheep-track's maze
The viewless snow-mist weaves a glist'ning haze,
Sees full before him, gliding without tread,
An image with a glory round its head;   30
The enamoured rustic worships its fair hues
Nor knows he makes the shadow he pursues!

Metrical Feet

LESSON FOR A BOY

Trōchĕe trīps frŏm lōng tŏ shōrt;
From long to long in solemn sort
Slōw Spōndēe stālks; strōng fŏot! yet ill able
Ēvĕr to cōme ŭp wĭth Dāctўl trĭsўllăblĕ.
Ĭambĭcs mārch frŏm shŏrt tŏ lōng;—   5
Wĭth ă leāp ănd ă boūnd thĕ swĭft Ānăpæsts thrōng;
One syllable long, with one short at each side,
Ămphībrăchўs hāstes wĭth ă stātelў stride;—
Fīrst ănd lāst bēĭng lōng, mĭddlĕ shōrt, Ămphĭmācer
Strīkes hĭs thūndērĭng hoōfs līke ă proūd hĭgh-brĕd Rācer.   10

If Derwent be innocent, steady, and wise,
And delight in the things of earth, water, and skies;
Tender warmth at his heart, with these metres to show it,
With sound sense in his brains, may make Derwent a poet,—
May crown him with fame, and must win him the love   15
Of his father on earth and his Father above.
          My dear, dear child!
Could you stand upon Skiddaw, you would not from its whole
          ridge
See a man who so loves you as your fond S. T. COLERIDGE.

To William Wordsworth

COMPOSED ON THE NIGHT AFTER HIS RECITATION OF A
POEM ON THE GROWTH OF AN INDIVIDUAL MIND

Friend of the wise! and teacher of the good!
Into my heart have I received that lay
More than historic, that prophetic lay
Wherein (high theme by thee first sung aright)
Of the foundations and the building up   5
Of a Human Spirit thou hast dared to tell
What may be told, to the understanding mind
Revealable; and what within the mind
By vital breathings secret as the soul
Of vernal growth, oft quickens in the heart   10
Thoughts all too deep for words!—

                 Theme hard as high!
Of smiles spontaneous, and mysterious fears,
(The first-born they of Reason and twin-birth)
Of tides obedient to external force,
And currents self-determined, as might seem,   15
Or by some inner power; of moments awful,
Now in thy inner life, and now abroad,
When power streamed from thee, and thy soul received
The light reflected, as a light bestowed—
Of fancies fair, and milder hours of youth,   20
Hyblean murmurs of poetic thought
Industrious in its joy, in vales and glens
Native or outland, lakes and famous hills!

Or on the lonely high-road, when the stars
Were rising; or by secret mountain-streams,   25
The guides and the companions of thy way!

Of more than Fancy, of the Social Sense
Distending wide, and man beloved as man,
Where France in all her towns lay vibrating
Like some becalmed bark beneath the burst   30
Of Heaven's immediate thunder, when no cloud
Is visible, or shadow on the main.
For thou wert there, thine own brows garlanded,
Amid the tremor of a realm aglow,
Amid a mighty nation jubilant,   35
When from the general heart of human kind
Hope sprang forth like a full-born Deity!
——Of that dear Hope afflicted and struck down,
So summoned homeward, thenceforth calm and sure
From the dread watch-tower of man's absolute self,   40
With light unwaning on her eyes, to look
Far on—herself a glory to behold,
The Angel of the vision! Then (last strain)
Of Duty, chosen laws controlling choice,
Action and joy!—An Orphic song indeed,   45
A song divine of high and passionate thoughts
To their own music chanted!

                                  O great Bard!
Ere yet that last strain dying awed the air,
With steadfast eye I viewed thee in the choir
Of ever-enduring men. The truly great   50
Have all one age, and from one visible space
Shed influence! They, both in power and act,
Are permanent, and Time is not with them,
Save as it worketh for them, they in it.

Nor less a sacred roll, than those of old,   55
And to be placed, as they, with gradual fame
Among the archives of mankind, thy work
Makes audible a linked lay of Truth,
Of Truth profound a sweet continuous lay,
Not learnt, but native, her own natural notes!   60
Ah! as I listened with a heart forlorn,
The pulses of my being beat anew:
And even as life returns upon the drowned,
Life's joy rekindling roused a throng of pains—
Keen pangs of Love, awakening as a babe   65
Turbulent, with an outcry in the heart;
And fears self-willed, that shunned the eye of hope:
And hope that scarce would know itself from fear;
Sense of past youth, and manhood come in vain,
And genius given, and knowledge won in vain;   70
And all which I had culled in wood-walks wild,
And all which patient toil had reared, and all,
Commune with thee had opened out—but flowers
Strewed on my corse, and borne upon my bier,
In the same coffin, for the self-same grave!   75

    That way no more! and ill beseems it me,
Who came a welcomer in herald's guise,
Singing of glory, and futurity,
To wander back on such unhealthful road,
Plucking the poisons of self-harm! And ill   80
Such intertwine beseems triumphal wreaths
Strewed before thy advancing!

                        Nor do thou,
Sage Bard! impair the memory of that hour
Of thy communion with my nobler mind
By pity or grief, already felt too long!   85

Nor let my words import more blame than needs.
The tumult rose and ceased: for peace is nigh
Where wisdom's voice has found a listening heart.
Amid the howl of more than wintry storms,
The halcyon hears the voice of vernal hours   90
Already on the wing.

                    Eve following eve,
Dear tranquil time, when the sweet sense of Home
Is sweetest! moments for their own sake hailed
And more desired, more precious for thy song,
In silence listening, like a devout child,   95
My soul lay passive, by thy various strain
Driven as in surges now beneath the stars,
With momentary stars of my own birth,
Fair constellated foam,[1] still darting off
Into the darkness; now a tranquil sea,   100
Outspread and bright, yet swelling to the moon.

   And when—O Friend! my comforter and guide!
Strong in thyself, and powerful to give strength!—
Thy long sustained Song finally closed,
And thy deep voice had ceased—yet thou thyself   105
Wert still before my eyes, and round us both
That happy vision of beloved faces—
Scarce conscious, and yet conscious of its close
I sate, my being blended in one thought
(Thought was it? or aspiration? or resolve?)   110
Absorbed, yet hanging still upon the sound—
And when I rose, I found myself in prayer.

[1] 'A beautiful white cloud of foam at momentary intervals coursed by the side
of the vessel with a roar, and little stars of flame danced and sparkled and went
out in it: and every now and then light detachments of this white cloud-like
foam darted off from the vessel's side, each with its own small constellation, over
the sea, and scoured out of sight like a Tartar troop over a wilderness.'—*The
Friend*, p. 220.

Song

A sunny shaft did I behold,
  From sky to earth it slanted:
And poised therein a bird so bold—
  Sweet bird, thou wert enchanted!
He sank, he rose, he twinkled, he trolled   5
  Within that shaft of sunny mist;
His eyes of fire, his beak of gold,
  All else of amethyst!

And thus he sang: 'Adieu! adieu!
Love's dreams prove seldom true.   10
The blossoms, they make no delay:
The sparkling dew-drops will not stay.
    Sweet month of May,
      We must away;
        Far, far away!   15
        To day! to day!'

The Knight's Tomb

Where is the grave of Sir Arthur O'Kellyn?
Where may the grave of that good man be?—
By the side of a spring on the breast of Helvellyn,
Under the twigs of a young birch tree!

The oak that in summer was sweet to hear,   5
And rustled its leaves in the fall of the year,
And whistled and roared in the winter alone,
Is gone,—and the birch in its stead is grown.—
The Knight's bones are dust,
And his good sword rust;—   10
His soul is with the saints, I trust.

On Donne's Poetry

With Donne, whose muse on dromedary trots,
Wreathe iron pokers into true-love knots;
Rhyme's sturdy cripple, fancy's maze and clue,
Wit's forge and fire-blast, meaning's press and screw.

Fancy in Nubibus

OR THE POET IN THE CLOUDS

O! it is pleasant, with a heart at ease,
  Just after sunset, or by moonlight skies,
To make the shifting clouds be what you please,
  Or let the easily persuaded eyes
Own each quaint likeness issuing from the mould   5
  Of a friend's fancy; or with head bent low
And cheek aslant see rivers flow of gold
  'Twixt crimson banks; and then, a traveller, go
From mount to mount through Cloudland, gorgeous land!

Or list'ning to the tide, with closed sight,   10
Be that blind bard, who on the Chian strand
  By those deep sounds possessed with inward light,
Beheld the Iliad and the Odyssee
  Rise to the swelling of the voiceful sea.

Youth and Age

Verse, a breeze mid blossoms straying,
Where Hope clung feeding, like a bee—
Both were mine! Life went a maying
            With Nature, Hope, and Poesy,
                        When I was young!   5
When I was young?—Ah, woful when!
Ah! for the change 'twixt Now and Then!
This breathing house not built with hands,
This body that does me grievous wrong,
O'er aery cliffs and glittering sands,   10
How lightly then it flashed along:—
Like those trim skiffs, unknown of yore,
On winding lakes and rivers wide,
That ask no aid of sail or oar,
That fear no spite of wind or tide!   15
Nought cared this body for wind or weather
When Youth and I liv'd in't together.

Flowers are lovely; Love is flower-like;
Friendship is a sheltering tree;
O! the joys, that came down shower-like,   20
Of Friendship, Love, and Liberty,
                        Ere I was old!

Ere I was old? Ah woful Ere,
Which tells me, Youth's no longer here!
O Youth! for years so many and sweet,   25
'Tis known, that Thou and I were one,
I'll think it but a fond conceit—
It cannot be, that Thou art gone!
Thy vesper-bell hath not yet toll'd:—
And thou wert aye a masker bold!   30
What strange disguise hast now put on,
To make believe, that Thou art gone?
I see these locks in silvery slips,
This drooping gait, this altered size:
But springtide blossoms on thy lips,   35
And tears take sunshine from thine eyes!
Life is but thought: so think I will
That Youth and I are house-mates still.

Dew-drops are the gems of morning,
But the tears of mournful eve!   40
Where no hope is, life's a warning
That only serves to make us grieve,
                        When we are old:
That only serves to make us grieve
With oft and tedious taking-leave,   45
Like some poor nigh-related guest,
That may not rudely be dismist;
Yet hath outstay'd his welcome while,
And tells the jest without the smile.

The Delinquent Travellers

Some are home-sick—some two or three,
Their third year on the Arctic Sea—
Brave Captain Lyon tells us so—
Spite of those charming Esquimaux.
But O, what scores are sick of Home,   5
Agog for Paris or for Rome!
Nay! tho' contented to abide,
You should prefer your own fireside;
Yet since grim War has ceas'd its madding,
And Peace has set John Bull agadding,   10
'Twould such a vulgar taste betray,
For very shame you must away!
'What? not yet seen the coast of France!
The folks will swear, for lack of bail,
You've spent your last five years in jail!'   15

Keep moving! Steam, or Gas, or Stage,
Hold, cabin, steerage, hencoop's cage—
Tour, Journey, Voyage, Lounge, Ride, Walk,
Skim, Sketch, Excursion, Travel-talk—
For move you must! 'Tis now the rage,   20
The law and fashion of the Age.
If you but perch, where Dover tallies,
So strangely with the coast of Calais,
With a good glass and knowing look,
You'll soon get matter for a book!   25
Or else, in Gas-car, take your chance
Like that adventurous king of France,

Who, once, with twenty thousand men
Went up—and then came down again;
At least, he moved if nothing more: 30
And if there's nought left to explore,
Yet while your well-greased wheels keep spinning,
The traveller's honoured name you're winning,
And, snug as Jonas in the Whale,
You may loll back and dream a tale.   35
Move, or be moved—there's no protection,
Our Mother Earth has ta'en the infection—
(That rogue Copernicus, 'tis said
First put the whirring in her head,)
A planet She, and can't endure   40
T'exist without her annual Tour:
The *name* were else a mere misnomer,
Since Planet is but Greek for *Roamer*.
The atmosphere, too, can do no less
Than ventilate her emptiness,   45
Bilks turn-pike gates, for no one cares,
And gives herself a thousand airs—
While streams and shopkeepers, we see,
Will have their run toward the sea—
And if, meantime, like old King Log,   50
Or ass with tether and a clog,
Must graze at home! to yawn and bray
'I guess we shall have rain to-day!'
Nor clog nor tether can be worse
Than the dead palsy of the purse.   55
Money, I've heard a wise man say,
Makes herself wings and flys away:
Ah! would She take it in her head
To make a pair for me instead!
At all events, the Fancy's free,   60
No traveller so bold as she.

From Fear and Poverty released
I'll saddle Pegasus, at least,
And when she's seated to her mind,
I within I can mount behind: 65
And since this outward I, you know,
Must stay because he cannot go,
My fellow-travellers shall be they
Who go because they cannot stay—
Rogues, rascals, sharpers, blanks and prizes,   70
Delinquents of all sorts and sizes,
Fraudulent bankrupts, Knights burglarious,
And demireps of means precarious—
All whom Law thwarted, Arms or Arts,
Compel to visit foreign parts,   75
All hail! No compliments, I pray,
I'll follow where you lead the way!
But ere we cross the main once more,
Methinks, along my native shore,
Dismounting from my steed I'll stray   80
Beneath the cliffs of Dumpton Bay,
Where, Ramsgate and Broadstairs between,
Rude caves and grated doors are seen:
And here I'll watch till break of day,
(For Fancy in her magic might   85
Can turn broad noon to starless night!)
When lo! methinks a sudden band
Of smock-clad smugglers round me stand.
Denials, oaths, in vain I try,
At once they gag me for a spy,   90
And stow me in the boat hard by.
Suppose us fairly now afloat,
Till Boulogne mouth receives our Boat.
But, bless us! what a numerous band
Of cockneys anglicise the strand!   95

Delinquent bankrupts, leg-bail'd debtors,
Some for the news, and some for letters—
With hungry look and tarnished dress,
French shrugs and British surliness.
Sick of the country for their sake   100
Of them and France *French leave* I take—
And lo! a transport comes in view
I hear the merry motley crew,
Well skill'd in pocket to make entry,
Of Dieman's Land the elected Gentry,   105
And founders of Australian Races.—
The Rogues! I see it in their faces!
Receive me, Lads! I'll go with you,
Hunt the black swan and kangaroo,
And that New Holland we'll presume   110
Old England with some elbow-room.
Across the mountains we will roam,
And each man make himself a home:
Or, if old hàbits ne'er forsaking,
Like clock-work of the Devil's making,   115
Ourselves inveterate rogues should be,
We'll have a virtuous progeny;
And on the dunghill of our vices
Raise human pine-apples and spices.
Of all the children of John Bull   120
With empty heads and bellies full,
Who ramble East, West, North and South,
With leaky purse and open mouth,
In search of varieties exotic
The usefullest and most patriotic,   125
And merriest, too, believe me, Sirs!
Are your Delinquent Travellers!

Work without Hope

LINES COMPOSED 21ST FEBRUARY 1827

All Nature seems at work. Slugs leave their lair—
The bees are stirring—birds are on the wing—
And Winter slumbering in the open air,
Wears on his smiling face a dream of Spring!
And I, the while, the sole unbusy thing,   5
Nor honey make, nor pair, nor build, nor sing.

Yet well I ken the banks where amaranths blow,
Have traced the fount whence streams of nectar flow.
Bloom, O ye amaranths! bloom for whom ye may,
For me ye bloom not! Glide, rich streams, away!   10
With lips unbrightened, wreathless brow, I stroll:
And would you learn the spells that drowse my soul?
Work without hope draws nectar in a sieve,
And hope without an object cannot live.

Duty Surviving Self-Love

THE ONLY SURE FRIEND OF DECLINING LIFE.
A SOLILOQUY

Unchanged within to see all changed without
Is a blank lot and hard to bear, no doubt.
Yet why at others' wanings should'st thou fret?
Then only might'st thou feel a just regret,

Hadst thou withheld thy love or hid thy light   5
In selfish forethought of neglect and slight.
O wiselier then, from feeble yearnings freed,
While, and on whom, thou may'st—shine on! nor heed
Whether the object by reflected light
Return thy radiance or absorb it quite: 10
And though thou notest from thy safe recess
Old friends burn dim, like lamps in noisome air,
Love them for what they are; nor love them less,
Because to thee they are not what they were.

Epitaph

Stop, Christian Passer-by!—Stop, child of God,
And read with gentle breast. Beneath this sod
A poet lies, or that which once seem'd he.—
O, lift one thought in prayer for S. T. C.;
That he who many a year with toil of breath   5
Found death in life, may here find life in death!
Mercy for praise—to be forgiven for fame
He ask'd, and hoped, through Christ. Do thou the same!

Fragments

1

Sea-ward, white gleaming thro' the busy scud
With arching Wings, the sea-mew o'er my head
Posts on, as bent on speed, now passaging
Edges the stiffer Breeze, now, yielding, drifts,
Now floats upon the air, and sends from far   5
A wildly-wailing Note.

2

I know 'tis but a dream, yet feel more anguish
Than if 'twere truth. It has been often so:
Must I die under it? Is no one near?
Will no one hear these stifled groans and wake me?

[? 1803]

3

What never is, but only is to be
This is not Life:—
O hopeless Hope, and Death's Hypocrisy!
And with perpetual promise breaks its promises.

[1804–5]

4

'Twas not a mist, nor was it quite a cloud,
But it pass'd smoothly on towards the sea—
Smoothly and lightly between Earth and Heaven:
                 So, thin a cloud,
It scarce bedimm'd the star that shone behind it: 5
                And Hesper now
Paus'd on the welkin blue, and cloudless brink,
A golden circlet! while the Star of Jove—
That other lovely star—high o'er my head
Shone whitely in the centre of his Haze   10
           . . . one black-blue cloud
Stretch'd, like the heaven, o'er all the cope of Heaven.

                               [1797]

Come, come thou bleak December wind,
   And blow the dry leaves from the tree!
Flash, like a love-thought, thro' me, Death!
   And take a life that wearies me.

                               [1806]

Let Eagle bid the Tortoise sunward soar—
As vainly Strength speaks to a broken Mind.

                               [1806]

You mould my Hopes you fashion me within:
And to the leading love-throb in the heart,
Through all my being, through my pulses beat;
You lie in all my many thoughts like Light,
Like the fair light of Dawn, or summer Eve,   5
On rippling stream, or cloud-reflecting lake;
And looking to the Heaven that bends above you,
How oft! I bless the lot that made me love you.

[1807]

The spruce and limber yellow-hammer
In the dawn of spring and sultry summer,
In hedge or tree the hours beguiling
With notes as of one who brass is filing.

[1807]

Two wedded hearts, if ere were such,
Imprison'd in adjoining cells,
Across whose thin partition-wall
The builder left one narrow rent,
And where, most content in discontent,   5
A joy with itself at strife—
Die into an intenser life.

[1808]

               I have experienced
The worst the world can wreak on me—the worst
That can make Life indifferent, yet disturb
With whisper'd discontent the dying prayer—
I have beheld the whole of all, wherein   5
My heart had any interest in this life
To be disrent and torn from off my Hopes
That nothing now is left. Why then live on?
That hostage that the world had in its keeping
Given by me as a pledge that I would live—   10
That hope of Her, say rather that pure Faith
In her fix'd Love, which held me to keep truce
With the tyranny of Life—is gone, ah! whither?
What boots it to reply? 'tis gone! and now
Well may I break this Pact, this league of Blood   15
That ties me to myself—and break I shall.

                             [1810]

11

The Netherlands

Water and windmills, greenness, Islets green;—
Willows whose Trunks beside the shadows stood
Of their own higher half, and willowy swamp:—
Farmhouses that at anchor seem'd—in the inland sky
The fog-transfixing Spires—   5
Water, wide water, greenness and green banks,
And water seen—

                             [1828]

I stand alone, nor tho' my heart should break,
Have I, to whom I may complain or speak.
Here I stand, a hopeless man and sad,
Who hoped to have seen my Love, my Life.
And strange it were indeed, could I be glad   5
Remembericg her, my soul's betrothéd wife.
For in this world no creatnre that has life
Was e'er to me so gracious and so good.
Her loss is to my Heart, like that Heart's blood.

NOTES

1. SONNET: TO THE AUTUMNAL MOON   1788

Written when he was sixteen, this is one of the earliest examples of Coleridge's lifelong preoccupation with the moon, and with the theme of hope and despair. The invocation, or apostrophe, of the first two lines is an eighteenth-century poetic device from which he never entirely freed himself.

1. DESTRUCTION OF THE BASTILLE   1789

The storming of the Bastille Prison in Paris on 14th July 1789 and the freeing of its political and other prisoners was hailed throughout Europe as a landmark in the destruction of despotism and the progress towards universal liberty. These lines—magniloquent as they are, in the manner of Gray's Pindaric odes—are interesting as showing the instantaneous enthusiasm with which young men of that date received the news of the outbreak of the French Revolution.

3. MONODY ON THE DEATH OF CHATTERTON   1790

Thomas Chatterton, posthumous son of a Bristol schoolmaster, was born in 1752. He tried to earn a living by fabricating medieval poems and satires and passing them off as genuine. Despite this fabrication, he had poetic genius. He went up to London in 1770, and poisoned himself in the same year owing to poverty and despair. His life and death later aroused the pity and indignation of the generous-minded. At eighteen the young and hopeful Coleridge compares his case with that of Chatterton.

16. *Butler:* Samuel Butler (1612–1680), author of *Hudibras* and other satirical works, died in poverty.

19. *Otway:* Thomas Otway (1652–1685), dramatist and author of *Venice Preserved,* also died in destitution.

25. *Avon:* the river on which Bristol stands.

6. PAIN   1790

Coleridge suffered even in childhood from rheumatism and dysentery, and all his life underwent much bodily pain.

7. GENEVIEVE   1789–90

At Christ's Hospital Coleridge spent about half of his eighteenth year in the sick ward. It is believed that 'Genevieve' was the daughter of a nurse, Mrs. Brewman. This and the previous poem refer to this period of sickness.

7. INSIDE THE COACH   1791

An example of the light, occasional verse Coleridge turned out readily all his life. Of these lines he wrote: 'Travelling in the Exeter Coach with three other passengers over Bagshot Heath, after some vain endeavours to compose myself I composed this Ode—August 17, 1791.'

8. A WISH   1792

One of three short poems included in a letter to Mary Evans written from Cambridge in February 1792.

9. SONNET: TO THE RIVER OTTER   ?1793

Coleridge's birthplace, Ottery St. Mary, was by the River Otter in Devon.

10. THE SIGH   1794

Included in a letter to Southey in November 1794, this records the lingering feeling for Mary Evans which Coleridge experienced even after the decision had been made to marry Sara Fricker and go with Southey and Edith Fricker to establish Pantisocracy in America.

11. PANTISOCRACY   1794

See Introduction, p. xi.

11. ON A DISCOVERY MADE TOO LATE   1794

Included in a letter to Southey in October 1794, this sonnet is an attempt at relief from the misery of knowing that he was in love with Mary Evans but committed to marry Sara Fricker and emigrate to America. Immediately following the sonnet is his well-known comment: 'When a man is unhappy, he writes damned bad poetry, I find.'

12. MELANCHOLY   ?1794

There is doubt as to the date of composition.

6. *adder's tongue:* usually called hart's tongue.

13. TO A YOUNG ASS   1794

11–12. *the thousand aches . . . :* misquoted from *Hamlet,* III. i. 73–74.

14. TO THE NIGHTINGALE   1795

Written shortly before his marriage to Sara Fricker, this is one of the few poems in which Coleridge writes of her in this romantic strain.

16. THE EOLIAN HARP   1795

The Aeolian Harp was an outdoor musical instrument very popular at this time. It consisted essentially of a number of strings stretched across a sounding board so that when the wind blew across it with varying intensity a vague wailing music was heard, not unlike the sound from telegraph wires. Coleridge used the instrument as a metaphor for the human spirit stirred by the wind of inspiration. In the poem his thoughts, straying like the wind on the instrument, lead him in the direction of a not strictly orthodox view of life, until he is recalled by Sara to a sense of simple Christian piety.

18. THIS LIME-TREE BOWER MY PRISON   1797

This poem marks the beginning of Coleridge's great period. It was first included in a letter to Southey dated 17th July 1797, with the following introductory sentences:

Charles Lamb has been with me for a week—he left me Friday morning.—The second day after Wordsworth came to me, dear

Sara accidentally emptied a skillet of boiling milk on my foot, which confined me during the whole time of C. Lamb's stay & still prevents me from all walks longer than a furlong.— While Wordsworth, his Sister & C. Lamb were out one evening; sitting in the arbour of T. Poole's garden, which communicates with mine, I wrote these lines, with which I am pleased—

In the original version the reference to the accident was more direct:

> Well—they are gone: and here must I remain,
> Lam'd by the scathe of fire, lonely & faint. . . .

In line 68, the repeated phrase 'My gentle-hearted Charles' was originally 'My Sister & my Friends', but in later editions Coleridge cut out all references to the Wordsworths, from whom he became estranged.

31–32. *With sad yet patient soul*. . . . A reference to the curse of hereditary insanity in the Lamb family which was a shadow over Charles all his life. In September 1796 his sister Mary had killed their mother in a fit of insanity.

21. THE RIME OF THE ANCIENT MARINER   1797–98

[In the notes on this poem the numbers refer to the numbers of stanzas.]

Part I

SUMMARY. 1–5. Introduction: the Mariner begins his tale to the Wedding Guest.

6–12. The southward journey as far as the Antarctic Circle. In 7 the southward direction of the voyage is indicated simply and economically.

In 8–9 the interruption by the Wedding Guest makes it unnecessary to describe the southward journey through the tropics.

13–20. The ship reaches the Antarctic and (18) rounds Cape Horn. The Albatross, symbol of spiritual good and a protection against ill-fortune, appeared dramatically in 14. The Mariner confesses to having killed it. Like every other part, Part I ends at a significant and dramatic moment.

136

Part II

SUMMARY. 1–4. The ship now sails northward (1). So far, all is well; the consequences of the Mariner's act are not apparent, and the sailors share the Mariner's guilt by approving his act.

5–14. The 'fair breeze' (i.e. Trade Winds) are succeeded by a dead calm as the ship reaches the equator from the south. J. L. Lowes quotes the description by Gilbert White, the naturalist, of the summer of 1783, which Coleridge would have experienced as a boy of nearly eleven:

> 'The summer of the year 1783 was an amazing and portentous one, and full of horrible phenomena; for . . . the peculiar haze, or smoky fog, that prevailed for many weeks in this island, . . . was a most extraordinary appearance, unlike anything known within the memory of man. . . . The sun, at noon, looked as blank as a clouded moon, and shed a rust-coloured ferruginous light on the ground, and floors of rooms; but was particularly lurid and blood-coloured at rising and setting. All the time the heat was . . . intense.'

The sailors silently accuse the Mariner, and the Albatross is hung round his neck. The 'cross' of 14 is usually taken to mean simply a crucifix, but it has been pointed out that it may refer, with greater symbolic force, to the 'mark of Cain'—that is, the cross branded on the foreheads of both Cain and the Wandering Jew, with both of whom the Mariner was associated in Coleridge's mind.

Part III

SUMMARY. The appearance of the skeleton ship with its crew of two, Death and Life-in-Death, dicing for the souls of the Mariner and the sailors. As the sun sets and the moon rises, the sailors drop dead, each with a parting curse for the Mariner.

The experience described in 4–5 is based on a personal memory of intense thirst during a walking tour in the Welsh mountains in 1794. So intense was the heat that Coleridge and the friends with him could not speak until they had found a puddle of water—after which they grinned at one another like idiots, as Coleridge later related.

Coleridge is sometimes accused of describing in 14 a physical impossibility, but members of the Royal Society were at this time discussing what was described as 'An Appearance of Light, Like a Star, seen in the dark Part of the Moon, on Friday the 7th of March, 1794'. (Philosophical Transactions of the Royal Society, 1794.)

Part IV

SUMMARY. 1–9. The abrupt and momentary re-introduction of the Wedding Guest marks the transition from the death of the sailors to the Mariner's solitary agony. The Mariner undergoes a spiritual death, isolated from both God and God's creation.

10–15. The appearance of the moon, as always in Coleridge, is a sign of spiritual regeneration. The creatures previously seen as disgusting ('slimy things') now appear beautiful and joyous ('happy living things'). A spontaneous impulse of love towards them in the Mariner's heart makes him bless them; and as a sign that the load of guilt is lifting, the Albatross falls from his neck.

In the description of the water-snakes (12) there is a reminiscence of the Bible not noted by Lowes in *The Road to Xanadu*. The account of Leviathan in *Job* contains the following: 'He maketh a path to shine after him; one would think the deep to be hoary.' (XLI. 32.) The word 'flakes' (12. 4) may be a reminiscence of *Job* XLI. 23: 'The flakes of his flesh are joined together.'

Part V

SUMMARY. 1–5. Sleep is sent as a gift from heaven, and rain ends the drought.

6–22. There is a storm; the ship begins to move, but not by natural means. Angelic spirits enter the bodies of the sailors and work the ship; the motive force is supplied by the polar spirit, still seeking vengeance for the murder of the Albatross, which had been under his protection.

23–26. In a fainting fit the Mariner overhears two spirit-voices, one of which declares that he must do further penance.

2. 1. *silly:* simple. (An archaism derived from the old ballads.)

16. 5. *jargoning:* cf. Chaucer, *Romaunt of the Rose*—

Layis of love full wel souning
Thei songin in ther jargoning.

Part VI

SUMMARY. 1–6. The ship is driven on by supernatural force. Its movement is not described directly, but commented on by the two spirit-voices.

7–15. Freed from the curse in the eyes of the dead sailors, the Mariner feels a fresh and invigorating breeze, as the ship speeds on to within sight of its home port.

16–23. As the ship enters the harbour in a brilliant moonlit calm, the angelic spirits leave the bodies of the dead sailors.

24–26. A pilot boat appears; the Mariner hears the voice of a Hermit, from whom he immediately decides to seek shrift for his crime.

Part VII

SUMMARY. 1–8. As the Pilot, his boy, and the Hermit reach the ship, full of apprehension at its mysterious appearance, there is a loud noise and the ship sinks.

9–12. The Mariner is saved by the Pilot's boat; the boy loses his wits at what he takes to be an appearance of the devil.

13–25. Once more on firm land, the Mariner begs the Hermit to shrive him, and he is constrained by an inner agony to tell his story for the first time. Thenceforward, at every recurrence of the same agony, the Mariner has to repeat the story, as soon as he recognizes the right listener. With the wedding feast in progress, the Mariner takes his leave of the Wedding Guest, who is too stunned to take any further part in the festivities.

---

44. ON A RUINED HOUSE IN A ROMANTIC COUNTRY   1797

This version of *The House that Jack Built* in a style of high-flown rhetoric was published under the pseudonym of Nehemiah Higginbottom as a parody of Coleridge's own early manner, which he now despised.

---

45. CHRISTABEL   1798–99

Perhaps the most famous unfinished poem in English, *Christabel* was begun in 1798, Part II was written in 1799, and several vain attempts were made to finish it later. Coleridge gave various reasons for his failure to finish it, but it seems clear that the real reason was simply that the subject itself afforded no inevitable poetic solution. Parts I and II were first published in 1816, together with *Kubla Khan* and *The Pains of Sleep*.

Part I is superior to Part II, and very different in atmosphere. Indeed, the chief attraction of the poem lies in the power and skill with which Coleridge evokes a brooding and sinister atmosphere in a medieval setting. We can only guess at the evil nature of Geraldine, but the whole poem is so charged with nameless horror that its first reviewers found it obscene and disgusting. Its influence, however, went far beyond its success; undoubtedly it was one of the first examples of the gothic-romantic element in English poetry which can be traced through Scott and Keats to Tennyson and the Pre-Raphaelites.

Whatever the extent of Coleridge's failure to work out the narrative part of his poem, there can be no doubt of the suggestive power of the lyrical aspects, especially in the opening. In achieving this, Coleridge was indebted to his own and Dorothy Wordsworth's observations of nature: compare lines 16–17 with the following entry in Dorothy's Journal for 25th January 1798:

'The sky spread over with one continuous cloud, whitened by the light of the moon.'

Compare also lines 49–50 with an entry for 7th March 1798:

'One only leaf upon the top of a tree—the sole remaining leaf—danced round and round like a rag blown by the wind.'

68. FROST AT MIDNIGHT   1798

Written in the cottage at Nether Stowey, where the contemplation of his sleeping child, Berkeley (born in 1797) leads him to revert to his own childhood at Christ's Hospital in London.

70. LEWTI   1798

First published pseudonymously in the *Morning Post* on 13th April 1798, it was to have been included in *Lyrical Ballads*, but was withdrawn at the last minute, and Coleridge himself adopted an apologetic tone about the poem: it was evidently he who wrote the note attached to it in the *Morning Post*, from which the following is quoted:

'Amidst images of war and woe, amidst scenes of carnage and horror of devastation and dismay, it may afford the mind a temporary relief to wander to the magic haunts of the Muses, to bowers and fountains which the despoiling powers of war have never visited, and where the lover pours forth his complaint, or receives the recompense of his constancy. The whole of the subsequent Love Chant is in a warm and impassioned strain. The fifth and last stanzas are, we think, the best.'

The poem in its original version was inspired by Mary Evans, with whom Coleridge was in love before his marriage. The name 'Lewti' originally appeared as 'Mary'.

73. FEARS IN SOLITUDE   1798

Written at Nether Stowey in April 1798, these lines express Coleridge's intense patriotism and his deep and simple love of the English countryside. For some time England had been alone in the war with France, and the threat of invasion remained a very real one at least until the victory at Trafalgar in 1805.

81. THE NIGHTINGALE   1798

Written in April 1798, this was sent in a letter to Wordsworth in May with the following lines:

> In stale blank verse a subject stale
> I send *per post* my *Nightingale*;
> And like an honest bard, dear Wordsworth,
> You'll tell me what you think, my Bird's worth.
> My opinion's briefly this—
> His *bill* he opens not amiss;
> And when he has sung a stave or so,
> His breast, & some small space below,
> So throbs & swells, that you might swear
> No vulgar music's working there.
> So far, so good; but then, 'od rot him!
> There's something falls off at his bottom.
> Yet, sure, no wonder it should breed
> That my Bird's Tail's a tail indeed

And makes its own inglorious harmony
Aeolio crepitû non carmine.

The Nightingale was included in *Lyrical Ballads.*

13. '*Most musical, most melancholy*': quoted from Milton, *Il Penseroso.*
40. *My Friend, and thou, our Sister:* William and Dorothy Wordsworth.
91. *My dear babe:* Hartley Coleridge, born 1796.

85. KUBLA KHAN   1798

The accepted date is May 1798, but a strong case has been made out
for October 1797. In any event *Kubla Khan* belongs to Coleridge's
greatest creative period.

Coleridge himself does not seem to have known what to make of
his own creation, for he did not publish it till 1816, when it appeared
in a volume with *Christabel* and *The Pains of Sleep*, prefaced by the
following note:

KUBLA KHAN
Or, a Vision in a Dream. A Fragment.

The following fragment is here published at the request of a poet
of great and deserved celebrity [Lord Byron], and, as far as the
Author's own opinions are concerned, rather as a psychological
curiosity, than on the ground of any supposed *poetic* merits.

In the summer of the year 1797, the Author, then in ill health,
had retired to a lonely farm-house between Porlock and Linton, on
the Exmoor confines of Somerset and Devonshire. In consequence
of a slight indisposition, an anodyne had been prescribed, from the
effects of which he fell asleep in his chair at the moment that he was
reading the following sentence, or words of the same substance, in
'Purchas's Pilgrimage': 'Here the Khan Kubla commanded a palace
to be built, and a stately garden thereunto. And thus ten miles of
fertile ground were enclosed with a wall.' The Author continued
for about three hours in a profound sleep, at least of the external
senses, during which time he has the most vivid confidence, that he
could not have composed less than from two to three hundred lines;
if that indeed can be called composition in which all the images rose
up before him as *things*, with a parallel production of the corre-

spondent expressions, without any sensation or consciousness of effort. On awaking he appeared to himself to have a distinct recollection of the whole, and taking his pen, ink, and paper, instantly and eagerly wrote down the lines that are here preserved. At this moment he was unfortunately called out by a person on business from Porlock, and detained by him above an hour, and on his return to his room, found, to his no small surprise and mortification, that though he still retained some vague and dim recollection of the general purport of the vision, yet, with the exception of some eight or ten scattered lines and images, all the rest had passed away like the images on the surface of a stream into which a stone has been cast, but, alas! without the after-restoration of the latter! . . .

It was typical of Coleridge to adopt an apologetic and self-depreciatory tone about a poem to which he feared the conventional response might be hostile. This response was expressed in a letter from his wife to Thomas Poole following the publication. In all her literary judgements Mrs. Coleridge echoed her brother-in-law, the ultra-conventional Robert Southey, Poet Laureate. She wrote: 'He [Coleridge] has been so unwise as to publish his fragments of "Christabel" & "Koula-Khan" . . . we were all sadly vexed when we read the advertizement of these things.'

A more sensitive and intelligent reaction was that of Charles Lamb, whose judgement has on the whole been that of posterity. Writing to Wordsworth in April 1816, he said: 'Coleridge is printing Xtabel, by Ld Byron's recommendation to Murray, with what he calls a vision, Kubla Khan—which said vision he repeats so enchantingly that it irradiates and brings heaven and Elusian bowers into my parlour while he sings or says it, but there is an observation "Never tell thy dreams", and I am almost afraid that Kubla Khan is an owl that won't bear day light, I fear lest it should be discovered by the lantern of typography and clear reducting to letters, no better than nonsense or no sense.' It was in this same letter that, speaking of Coleridge as an opium-addict under the care of Dr. Gillman at Highgate, he said: 'He is very bad, but then he wonderfully picks up another day, and his face when he repeats his verses hath its ancient glory, an Archangel a little damaged.'

The implication in Lamb's remarks that *Kubla Khan* is a sort of sonorous nonsense is given some support by Coleridge's own account of the poem, in which he speaks of it as a 'psychological curiosity', a 'fragment' sponsored by Lord Byron, and the product of a trance; but much of this should undoubtedly be discounted. Humphrey House and other modern critics are right in regarding the poem as a single, unified whole, complete and coherent. According to House, '*Kubla Khan* is a poem about the act of poetic creation . . . a triumphant positive statement of the potentialities of poetry'. According to Lowes, Coleridge had been reading Bruce's account of his discovery of the sources of the Nile in Abyssinia. The Nile is transmuted to the River Alph of classical legend, which was sometimes identified with the Nile. Both rivers were sacred—the Nile because it is the source of all life in Egypt. It is here that Kubla, the legendary prince, raised his 'pleasure dome', symbol of perfect happiness on earth. At the end of the poem, writing of himself as the inspired bard in a frenzy of poetic exaltation, Coleridge asserts that he too could create this symbol of happiness if he could recover the poetry revealed to him in dreams.

Lowes accepted Coleridge's published account of the genesis of *Kubla Khan* because of the excellence of the last section: 'Nobody in his waking senses could have fabricated those amazing eighteen lines'. This is a quite untenable assertion; but in any case it is worth referring to Coleridge's note on the Crewe MS., thought by some to be of earlier date than the published text of 1816. Here he tells us that *Kubla Khan* was 'composed in a sort of Reverie'. This suggests a different and, I think, more probable genesis than the trance-like automatism assumed by some writers.

For a fuller discussion of the meaning of the poem, see Humphrey House: *Coleridge*, 1953.

87. LOVE   1799

First published with seven additional stanzas as the 'Introduction to the Tale of the Dark Ladie', a poem intended for the second edition of *Lyrical Ballads* but never finished. In October 1799 Coleridge had visited the Hutchinsons at Sockburn on the Tees, where he met for the first time Wordsworth's future sister-in-law, Sara. The idealized love he felt for her was expressed in this poem.

90. THE KEEPSAKE   ?1802

First published in the autumn of 1802, it may also have been written at this date, and not two years before, as earlier editors have suggested.

First published in December 1801 with two preliminary stanzas, later cancelled, referring to the futility and wickedness of public affairs.

93.   TO ASRA   1801

'Asra' was Coleridge's pseudonym for Sara Hutchinson. This sonnet was prefixed to a copy of *Christabel* which he presented to her. It was not published until 1893.

93.   LOVE'S SANCTUARY   ?1801

Like the preceding, this was inspired by Sara Hutchinson and was first published in 1893.

94.   DEJECTION: A LETTER   1802

This poem was written on 4th April 1802, and sent as a letter to Sara Hutchinson. Bound up with the expression of his sense of failure and frustration as a creative writer is the intimate revelation of Coleridge's personal unhappiness and his deep idealistic love for Sara.

Coleridge included in a letter to William Sotheby of 19th July 1802 what he called the 'introduction' to the poem, 'that being of a sufficiently general nature to be interesting to you'. He omitted the personal revelations and substituted 'Wordsworth' or 'William' for 'Sara'. For the purpose of publication the original poem of 340 lines was cut down and re-shaped to form the 139 lines of *Dejection: an Ode,* which was printed in the *Morning Post* for 4th October 1802, the day of Wordsworth's marriage to Mary Hutchinson. This version was preceded by the stanza from Sir Patrick Spens about the new moon with the old moon in her arms, and 'Sara' was replaced not by 'Wordsworth' but by a mythical 'Edmund'.

When Coleridge later included the ode in *Sybilline Leaves,* he printed a version also of 139 lines, with 'Lady' in place of 'Edmund', etc. This has become the received text.

I am convinced that since the original poem was first reprinted from the MS. in 1947, it must be accepted as the real poem, and immeasurably the best version available. I cannot agree with Mr. E. L. Griggs when he says, in his monumental edition of the letters (1956), that in reshaping *Dejection* 'he gave it a unity lacking in its epistolary form and omitted the most personal passages. Thus he turned a poetic letter full of self-revelation and self-pity into a work of art with a timeless and universal significance'.

The opinion of Humphrey House seems to me nearer the truth. He maintains that the received version, despite brilliant passages, lacks artistic unity, and that although the original version is not fully coherent, it has far greater unity. Poetically the Ode is a maimed version of the Letter. 'The treatment of his poems too much as embryo philosophy,' House concludes, 'has tended to obscure the place of the affections and feelings in them.' (See the whole of this interesting discussion in *Coleridge*, pp. 133–141.)

Self-pity is only one of the emotional elements in the poem. There is no evidence that Coleridge printed any of the revised versions of the original poem by choice rather than from necessity. The original has an organic wholeness and a complexity unequalled in any of the shorter versions. There is an interplay of personal emotion, general speculation, and external stimulus which is lost if the poem is shortened. The warm and intimate, yet idealistic, passion for Sara is the poem's very centre, and round it all the other elements fall naturally into place. In order to suggest this essential unity, a unity perhaps more complete than even House allowed, I give here a brief and bald summary of the argument:

1–43. 'A grief without a pang' inhibits the full experience of the beauty of the evening.

44–51. I must not look to the external world to supply my lack of inner joy.

52–73. There is no joy even in the thought of you, Sara, looking at the moon, as I am doing, even though such a vision was part of my boyhood musings.

74–98. Although I would prefer to think of you in the haunts where we were happy together, yet it is a pleasure to think of you looking at the moon and thinking sympathetically of me.

99–129. This evening reminds me of my extreme happiness one evening with your sister Mary and you. Why did I not think of this when I wrote you the letter which made you ill?

130–168. I wish you joy in the same household as William, Mary and Dorothy—of which I can never be a member. To know you happy is better for me than to see you and know that I can never share your happiness.

169–215. Yet the thought of your being ill and me absent turns my mind to the storm now raging outside. The storm-wind inspires my own imagination.

216–230. A blessing on Sara and a prayer for her recovery. (The line 'And be this Tempest but a Mountain Birth!' means simply, 'May the storm come to nothing after all': the reference is to the Latin line about the mountain labouring and bringing forth a mouse.)

231–271. I was once full of joy and hope, but now distresses weigh upon me and rob me of creative power. I am not speaking now of my domestic unhappiness; but what makes me grieve is that when you and those I love are unhappy, I have no ready and natural sympathy to offer, because my way of life has frozen up my humanity at its source.

272–340. Even my children, whom I love, are a source of sorrow; and the beauty of nature is no longer a solace. For we only get from nature what we give. The whole world derives its beauty only from the joy in our own souls. The essence of joy is innocence—our innocent love shall remake heaven and earth for us—and you, amidst those you love, will enjoy an innocent happiness.

105.   THE PICTURE   1802

Only the first 25 lines of this long, rambling, and uneven poem are here given. With the sub-title 'The Lover's Resolution', the poem as a whole was first published in the *Morning Post* for 6th September 1802.

107.   A DAY DREAM   1802

Addressed to Sara Hutchinson (Asra), this poem refers to the experience described in *Dejection* (99–107).

109.   THE PAINS OF SLEEP   1803

The earliest draft of these lines was sent in a letter to Southey in September 1803. The revised text was published with *Christabel* and *Kubla Khan* in 1816. Coleridge did not realize until later that the cause of his nightmares was the opium he had taken to relieve physical suffering. In the letter to Southey these lines occur immediately after the poem:

'I do not know how I came to scribble down these verses to you— my heart was aching, my head all confused—but they are, doggrels as they may be, a true portrait of my nights.—What to do, I am at a loss:—for it is hard thus to be withered, having the faculties & attainments, which I have.'

In a letter to Poole written a few days later Coleridge describes his state of mind and body thus:

'God forbid that my worst Enemy should ever have the Nights & the Sleeps that I have had, night after night—surprised by Sleep, while I struggled to remain awake, starting up to bless my own loud Screams that had awakened me—yea, dear friend! till my repeated Night-yells had made me a Nuisance in my own House. As I live & am a man, this is an unexaggerated Tale—my Dreams became the substances of my Life.'

III. PHANTOM   1805

These lines first appeared in a Malta notebook dated 1805. They illustrate the idea that love can exist independently of the outward circumstances of form and appearance. They evidently refer to one of Coleridge's first meetings with Sara Hutchinson, already alluded to in stanza 4 of *Love* (p. 87). The 'rifted stone' of *Phantom* may be 'the statue of the arméd knight', which has been identified as a figure in the church at Sockburn, the home of the Hutchinsons, which Coleridge first visited in 1799.

III. CONSTANCY TO AN IDEAL OBJECT   ?1804–1806

The date of thiss poem is doubtful. Line 18 suggests that Coleridge was abroad, possibly in Malta or Italy (1804–1806). Some editors assign a considerably later date. In these lines he contrasts the object of his love (supposedly Sara Hutchinson) with its idealized form in his mind. He knows that the ideal of a happy domestic life with her will never be realized. Has the ideal, then, no substance? No, for it is only the projection of himself, like the image cast before him by a man walking at dawn in a snow-mist. (Coleridge had witnessed this phenomenon himself, and had evidently been much impressed by it.)

112. METRICAL FEET 1806

This exercise, begun for Hartley and concluded for his brother Derwent, is sound advice for a poet—develop the moral and physical senses and the affections together with a mastery of technical detail.

114. TO WILLIAM WORDSWORTH 1807

The original version of these lines was written immediately after a recitation by Wordsworth of *The Prelude* in January 1807. When it was revised for publication ten years later, the more personal lines were cut out. The generous and unreserved praise of Wordsworth, however, was not in the least moderated, despite the estrangement of the poets. In the first 47 lines Coleridge sums up the themes of Wordsworth's poetic autobiography—his childhood and his adolescence, his visit to France at the time of the Revolution, and his return home disillusioned by the course of events in France since the first high hopes they had raised. He then (47–60) hails Wordsworth as one of the great poets of all time, and contrasts his own miserable failure (61–75). All his own gifts and the hopes he aroused are like flowers upon the grave of his early promise. Coleridge then reproves himself for indulging gloomy thoughts in the midst of his friend's triumph, and urges Wordsworth not to pity him since the recital of *The Prelude* has brought him peace of mind and renewed hope (76–112).

21. *Hyblaean:* bee-like.

33. *thine own brows garlanded:* Wordsworth himself rejoiced at the outbreak of the Revolution.

118. SONG: A SUNNY SHAFT DID I BEHOLD 1815

First published as a lyric in Coleridge's poetic drama about Hungarian history, *Zapolya* (1817).

118. THE KNIGHT'S TOMB ?1817

This may have been composed as a metrical experiment in combining dactylic lines with iambic. The date usually given in 1817 but, it may have been much earlier. It has been suggested that the lines were intended to form part of *Christabel*.

119. ON DONNE'S POETRY   ?1818

Coleridge was one of the first to appreciate the poetry of the Metaphysicals, who had been neglected during the eighteenth century.

119. FANCY IN NUBIBUS   1817

This sonnet recalls the references in *Hamlet, Antony and Cleopatra* and *The Tempest* to shapes in the clouds.

120. YOUTH AND AGE   1823–1832

Lines 1–43 were probably written in 1823 and 44–49 in 1832. Lines 1–38 were first published in 1828, and 39–49 in 1832. The poem as a whole first appeared in 1834.

122. THE DELINQUENT TRAVELLERS   1824

A good-natured satire contrasting ironically the fashionable travellers who flocked to the Continent as soon as the Napoleonic wars were over with the criminals who were transported to the penal settlements in Van Dieman's Land (Tasmania) and New Holland (Australia).

3. *Captain Lyon:* this refers to *The Private Journal of Captain G. F. Lyon, of his Majesty's Ship Hecla, during the recent Voyage of Discovery under Captain Parry* (1824).

81. *Dumpton Bay:* a coast village near Ramsgate, where Coleridge spent some weeks in 1824.

126. DUTY SURVIVING SELF-LOVE   1826

In the original MS. this was preceded by a note about the consolations of philosophy in old age: 'selfless Reason is the best Comforter, and only sure friend of declining Life.' Coleridge characteristically equates friendship with a lamp in a metaphor borrowed from contemporary science. He was a friend of Sir Humphrey Davy, inventor of the miner's safety lamp. (See line 12.)

127. EPITAPH 1833

In line 6 Coleridge specifically identifies himself with the Ancient Mariner, as he appears to have done previously in *Constancy to an Ideal Object*, lines 22–24.

128. FRAGMENTS

1.
From an undated MS.

2. ?1803
This fragment may have been written at the same period as *The Pains of Sleep*, to the subject of which it is clearly related.

3. 1804–05
A fragment from a MS. of the Malta period which evidently sums up Coleridge's state of mind at this time.

4. 1797
A fragment from a MS.

5. 1806
An adaptation of a stanza from Percy's version of *Waly, Waly, Love be bonny*:

> Marti'mas wind when wilt thou blaw,
>   And shake the green leaves aff the tree?
> O gentle death, when wilt thou cum?
>   For of my life I am wearie.

10. 1810
These lines from a MS. clearly refer to the death of any hopes Coleridge may have had of his love for Sara Hutchinson.

12.
These lines transcribed from the fly-leaf of a book are not certainly by Coleridge. If they are, they evidently belong to the same period as 9 ('I have experienced').

INDEX OF TITLES AND FIRST LINES

152